TALES OF A FUTURE CAT LADY

STARR, M.D.

CHERRY BLOSSOMS PUBLISHING

Copyright © 2021 by Starr, M.D.

All rights reserved.

No part of this book may be reproduced in any form or by any electronic or mechanical means, including information storage and retrieval systems, without written permission from the author, except for the use of brief quotations in a book review.

To my fellow square pegs,

You have been told you are too loud. You have been told you are too bold. You have been told that you are too proud. Too assertive. Too sexy. Too independent. Too you.
You have been told to soften. You have been told to fold into yourself so that you can fit into a world of round holes. I implore you; stay true to you. Embrace your edges and use what makes you different to carve out spaces of your own.

With love,
Starr, M.D.

CONTENTS

Foreword	vii
1. Italy Here We Come	1
2. Extra Spice and Daddy's Advice: What This Little Girl Was Made Of	10
3. Fast and Furious in Florence	17
4. Get out the kitchen	25
5. Go Big! Go Rome!	31
6. Sexual Recreation	39
7. These tears ain't for you	47
8. Lost and Found in Venice	54
9. Lively Loner	62
10. The Journey Home	70
11. One and Done	77
12. Rockstar	87
13. Daredevil	95
14. Recreational Use Only	102
15. Intimacy versus Isolation	110
16. The Longest One Night Stand Ever	119
17. Curiosity and the Cat Lady Trope	127
18. Tiger Mom	134
19. Life After Death	142
20. Fast Ass Lil' Girl	148
21. Scars	156
22. B's are Bad	163
23. Don't Be Pathetic	171
24. Lost Faith	177
25. Third Party Perceptions	185
26. Refuge	193
27. Everything but Domestic	201
28. Absorbing the Information	208
29. Sphinx and the Cat Lady	214

References	221
Acknowledgments	225
About the Author	227

FOREWORD

Rosalyn and I are childhood best friends. When she gave me the honor of writing her foreword, I was terrified. How do I describe in 500 words, someone that I have admired for decades? The only way to write about Rosalyn, is to be authentic.

When I first met Rosalyn, she was a confident spitfire, with a personality as voracious as her curly, fire-red hair. A metaphor personified; her hair represented the duality of her personality. Her long locks were wispy and soft to the touch, but the deep red hues warned of the dangers of a roaring internal fire. That's the enigma of Rosalyn. An iron-clad exterior that appears impenetrable, protecting the delicate vulnerabilities of an inner child that was full of love and wonder.

While most of her female peers were driven by emotions, Rosalyn was driven by an all-consuming determination, to achieve success and independence, at any cost, by any means necessary. Attending academically challenging schools, she lived by the mantra, "Books Before Boys, Because Boys Bring Babies."

There were expectations for her to get married and have children. Rosalyn, never one to conform to societal norms, trailblazed a life that was unconventional, on her own terms.

Rosalyn had beauty and brains and made no secret that she favored intelligence. When people suggested that she could be a model, she would quickly snap back, "Or a MD!".

Always an honor student, she graduated high school with enough credits to make a college freshman blush. Her academic prowess continued through university, medical school, and her medical residency, accumulating awards and promotions along the way, all while staying unapologetically authentic to her true self.

A world-traveler, collecting passport stamps, Rosalyn has circumvented the globe several times, spending time in exotic locales such as Bali, developing spiritual connections in Africa, and partying in Ibiza. This highly decorated surgeon welcomed life in the delivery room, while simultaneously celebrating life through experiences that most can only dream of having.

Her ability to quickly learn new languages and capture the hearts of people from different cultures, is like a chameleon. But Rosalyn doesn't blend in, she stands out. A flame, a shining light; people are drawn to her warmth, transparency, and authenticity.

If you have dared to live outside the box, are weighed down by society's expectations, or stuck in a life that no longer serves you, this book will provide encouragement to find your own way and the strength to resist mediocrity. You will find pieces yourself in the main character.

As you meet the actors and supporting characters, the exes, frenemies, the domineering authority figure, you will immediately recognize them as a character from your life. You will see how a decorated medical doctor goes from surgical scrubs to fishnets and thigh high boots without skipping a beat.

Settle in and get comfy, as Rosalyn shares her story on what it means to be human, to be inspired, and most of all, finding peace in being unapologetically, you.

1

ITALY HERE WE COME

You have got to be kidding me! Storming down the hallway towards the elevator, this thought repeated over and over in my mind as I punched the down button.

"I cannot fucking believe this!" I said aloud as the elevator doors opened. It was our first night in Italy and I was not expecting our romantic rendezvous to start like this. We were staying in Ravenna with plans to hop from one Italian city to the next in a quick tour of some of the country's most magical places. We both thought it would make for a fun way to spend our first vacation together. I entered the elevator and pressed the lobby button. Shaking my head in disgust during the descent, I thought about what transpired in our hotel room.

In preparation for fun days and sexy nights, I packed several pieces of lingerie. After our long day of travel, I slid into a tiny black sheer and lace teddy. I crawled into bed beside him, hoping he was just as eager to relax as I was. I pressed myself onto him and caressed my legs along his. Pushing my breasts against his body, I looked into his eyes and traced his skin gently with my fingertips. I leaned in to kiss him and as I closed my eyes and parted my lips he spoke.

"Hey!? Where is that word search puzzle book you had on the plane?"

I blinked. A breathless "huh" is the only response I could muster. He repeated his request.

"Do you really want that word search book right now?" I said slyly, as I adjusted my position giving him full view of my lace decorated body.

"Yep." He responded. I blinked again and again as if the fluttering of my lashes would rewind time and we would be well on our way to an intimate entanglement.

Recounting the events that led to my abrupt exit from the room, I barely noticed when the elevator stopped in the lobby. The lobby bar of the Grand Hotel Mattei in Ravenna was much brighter than a hotel lobby bar needed to be. The ultramodern white sofa and chairs with black trim scattered around the area were more trendy than comfortable. I took a seat near the back of the bar, distancing myself from the crowd. There were several groups of people milling about, chatting, and laughing as they sipped libations. They looked like they were having a great time or at the very least, they were having a lot more fun than I was. I motioned for the bartender.

"Vodka soda! Grazie!"

"Do you speak Italian?" He asked, his English perfect.

"No." I said with a smile. "All I can say is Ciao, Grazie, and Parli Inglese." We laughed. I drank and made small talk with the nice guy at the bar. Usually I hated small talk, but I was too furious to go back upstairs. While I entertained idle conversation, my inner thoughts began to drift. I had not envisioned our vacation having such a shaky start. Even more problematic is that I did not foresee us having a complete communication meltdown. Just the other day we were praising ourselves for how well we worked together and twelve hours in Italy was putting that statement to the test.

"Un Altro." I ordered another cocktail and recounted how we got here.

A LITTLE OVER FORTY-EIGHT HOURS AGO, I WAS ANXIOUSLY AND excitedly logging out of my computer to leave the office. Days at the office before taking time away were hectic and involved reviewing lab and imaging results, making patient phone calls, and ensuring patients with ongoing concerns had appropriate follow up. My workload was heavier than usual, compounded by playing catch up due to being away for two weddings in the weeks prior. Getting out of doctor mode and into vacation mode was a more than welcomed change of pace. I was desperately looking forward to this trip.

A light drizzle, a mixture of ice and rain, was starting to pick up as I ran to my car. Traffic was hectic as usual in Chicago, but the slow drive home was a blur. I was busy reviewing my pre-vacation mental checklist. I boarded my dog, Scrappy, a seven-pound Yorkie Chihuahua mix, that morning. Home visits had been set for Sox, my black tuxedo cat with white feet. Her litter box was clean, and her food and water dispensers were full. I was packed and had clothes for every occasion. I smiled, pleased with my productivity.

By the time I walked into my twenty-first floor, West Loop apartment I was confident all my pre-vacation affairs were in order. I collapsed onto the couch and allowed myself to relax. Moments later, I was hit with a wave of excitement. I loved to travel. In the last year I had been to five different countries. I had trekked rainforests and rappelled down hidden waterfalls in Costa Rica. I had celebrated my birthday in the Dominican Republic. I had reveled in Caribbean culture at the Caribbean Carnival in Toronto, Ontario, Canada. I had toured the Van Gogh museum, the Rijksmuseum, and the Heineken Factory in Amsterdam, Netherlands. I had drunk beer with people from all over the world during Oktoberfest in Munich, Germany. Exploring new venues, experiencing different cultures, and indulging in the spirited nightlife of foreign lands instilled within me an endless sense of childlike wonder. Everything about traveling from passing time at an airport bar to landing in a place where a new adventure awaits made me feel alive. Tomorrow I was off to Italy, but this trip contained an added element. I would be traveling as a "we".

It had been a while since I was in a relationship. I relished in the frivolous and superficial encounters I had and found most of my serious relationships suffocating. With my best friends settling down, I arbitrarily decided this was the year I would make a conscious effort to seek companionship. So far, my relationship with Kevin was different from the ones in my past, and I was excited. There was no guessing and no games. Instead, Kevin gave repeated assurances that he was "in it for the long haul". Such intense affirmations at early stages in relationships usually turned me off and turned my bullshit shield on. However, he insisted I had the set of characteristics that he never thought he would find in one woman. Having always been told I was different, I bought in. Even more interestingly was that this time I felt the same.

We met by happenstance. Kevin was interviewing for a management position in air traffic control at Chicago's O'Hare International Airport and I was returning from a wedding in my home state of Tennessee. Our connection was instant. He was well educated, a professional and military veteran, tall, had a handsome face, and a great physique. He lived in North Carolina but was determined we keep in contact. We did.

We spent hours on the phone talking, listening, and learning about one another. We connected over upward mobility in our chosen careers. I had recently accepted the position of Medical Director and Chair of the Department of Obstetrics and Gynecology and he was looking to advance in his career. Where many men had shied away when they discovered I was a doctor, Kevin's enthusiasm was palpable when I announced that I would be leading the department.

We bonded over hobbies, movies, the adrenaline rush of skydiving, and the serenity of scuba diving. His most attractive quality was that he wanted to try new things and craved excitement just as much as I did. Kevin told lame dad jokes and was corny, but I did not mind. I liked that he was comfortable being himself.

Our most interesting commonality was that neither of us had children. During one of our marathon conversations, he tentatively asked if I wanted children of my own. When my answer was no, there was an audible sigh of relief. He told me that he did not want children either. I laughed aloud and then we laughed together. We swapped horror stories about reactions we had received in the dating world once the subject of children came up. After one upping each other over and over, we laughed uncontrollably, and our bond was solidified.

It very soon became clear that we wanted the same things from life: adventure and an intimate partner with whom we could create and share those adventures. We marveled at the idea of incessant world travel and exploring uncharted locales together. We fantasized about finding hidden gems in those places and leaving our mark behind to be discovered. Given the obvious and much discussed mutual interest, we made plans to see each other again. Several months and many visits later, we decided to make Italy our first adventure.

Kevin was flying into Chicago and the following morning we would travel together to Italy. We would fly into Venice, drive to Ravenna, and then spend eight days on a road trip through the country. I snapped out of my daydream and checked my phone for the time. His flight would be arriving soon. I got off the couch and headed towards the airport.

After making several circles around the O'Hare arrivals terminal, I spotted Kevin walking towards the passenger pick up. A smile quickly spread across my lips as I pulled in closer. I popped the trunk and hopped out of the car. Kevin greeted me with a huge smile and an embrace. We lingered a while before heading off. The drive back to the West Loop was filled with banter about his flight and work. There was handholding and gentle affection. I was shocked by how happy I was to have him here. I enjoyed being alone and was quite content with the lifestyle I had cultivated for myself. I lived by the Horacio Jones quote "your presence has to feel better than my solitude." Kevin's presence felt good, and as we prepared for bed that night, he gave me a small gift, a congratulations on my promotion. I smiled and kissed him deeply and we allowed passion to overtake us.

After he had fallen asleep, I lay awake, my mind buzzing. The double weekend wedding whirlwind I was just a part of had been exhausting. Flying from Chicago to Nashville on two back-to-back weekends to be a bridesmaid in two different best friends' weddings, one with a two-part ceremony was no easy feat. Although the tight travel scheduled with days of work in between had been taxing, I loved getting to be a part of my friends' celebrations of love. My friends are my chosen family and each of those women are my sisters. Remembering the joy of those moments was overwhelming and had a dizzying effect as they washed over me. It was uncharacteristic for me to become consumed by a romantic fantasy, yet as I lay in bed next to Kevin, I found myself wondering, could this be my forever?

Kevin was a man with whom I shared similar beliefs. Someone who praised my strength, encouraged my ambitions, and celebrated my accomplishments. A man with whom I shared an undeniable chemistry and unspoken communication through touch and affection. I wanted to know more. I wanted to know everything. I was not a stranger to fiery yet fruitless exchanges with men, and most times it was I who cut the strings. I wanted things to be different with Kevin and hoped we were genuinely compatible. I knew in a few short hours we would find out. Travel has a way of doing that. I quelled my thoughts and allowed myself to fall asleep.

The alarm jolted me awake and I reached for my phone quickly to silence it. I rolled over and whispered good morning and was greeted with a kiss. Our journey to Italy was starting in a few hours and our flight itinerary left little wiggle room. The layover in Paris was just under forty minutes and navigating international airports can be tricky. We played around in bed for a bit until I insisted we get ready with a gentle reminder of Chicago traffic.

I was giddy the entire cab ride to the airport. His energy matched mine as we watched *American Idol* videos on my phone. We talked about planned activities and the sites we were most excited to see as LaPorsha Renee's voice crooned in the background. After arriving at the airport, we slowly made our way through the O'Hare security lines and navigated to our departure gate. Soon, it was wheels up. We giggled and gave each other a little peck as the plane started its ascent.

By the time we arrived in Italy, there was a palpable shift in Kevin's demeanor. His face, usually warm and inviting, was expressionless. I attributed the expression on his face, or lack thereof, to being tired. We had completed a long day of travel and still had the drive to Ravenna ahead. I pushed the observation to the back of my mind. Maybe, I was tired as well.

We hopped in the rental after throwing our bags in the trunk and got ready for the two-hour drive to Ravenna which was to be our base for most of the trip. It was a charming city to explore and a relatively short drive to Florence, Rome, and Venice. I closed the passenger side door and buckled my seatbelt. I looked over at him beaming. Ready to play DJ for our drive, I was about to take his song request when the question he asked next stopped the words from leaving my mouth.

"Have you always been so sassy?" The blankness on his face made the question colder than I assumed he intended.

My smile faded. I paused and swallowed hard. I had confirmed two things: one, something was indeed wrong and two, the look on his face was not secondary to fatigue. My mind raced as I wondered where his question had come from. Although this was not my first encounter with the word sassy, it usually came after I had made some quick-witted quip born out of defensiveness. In the professional setting its sister terms bold or audacious were used to describe me as a young administrator.

However, after making biting commentary or being a strong leader, I am prepared to be described as sassy. This time, the term caught me by surprise.

"Sassy?" I tilted my head like a cat confused by its owner's commands hoping to convey my complete and total lack of understanding. "What have I done to make you say that?" I asked calmly.

"It's just the way you say things." His response was curt, as if his statement on my demeanor was definitive and punctuated the end of the conversation. As someone who believed two adults in a relationship can and should communicate effectively, I disregarded the absoluteness of his words and sought answers.

"Can you be more specific? What did I say and when?" Truly seeking to understand and reconcile, I remained calm. I waited on his response with wide eyes and a partially open mouth. I no longer had to hope my confusion was evident. Flabbergasted was written all over my face.

"I don't have any specific examples." He snapped. The tension in my body started to rise and RP paced back and forth within.

"Well, next time you notice something, let me know in the moment." I managed a smile and attempted to sound more chipper than I felt. Although I was unsure about how we found ourselves debating my disposition, I was ready to smooth over this little road bump and get on with the trip. As I took a deep breath and relaxed my shoulders, Kevin again spoke.

"It's just the way you say things. It's how you talk to people. Your tone."

I considered his brief elaboration. I had interacted with a few waitresses and a rental car agent. A proponent of common courtesy, I was sure to use the phrases excuse me, please, and thank you any time I conducted any interactions with customer service individuals.

"But you can't give me any examples?" I asked with a hint of sarcasm in my words. Annoyed by the exchange, RP's voice overtook my own and added, "Have you considered it's how you have chosen to interpret things?"

He briskly turned to look at me, as if asking if *he* misperceived my actions was the most offensive question he had ever been asked. I shrugged and again calmly asked that he notify me in the moment if he noticed it again. He nodded. I connected my phone to the speakers and bopped happily to the soundtrack. Kevin remained silent for the rest of the drive, and although he did not speak another word, his question echoed in my mind.

"Have you *always* been so sassy?"

2

EXTRA SPICE AND DADDY'S ADVICE: WHAT THIS LITTLE GIRL WAS MADE OF

"No! There is not a Santa Claus!" I said assertively, hand on my hip and staring directly at Tia and RJ, my next-door neighbors. We were outside talking to each other through the chain link fence that separated our homes. Christmas was approaching and RJ was shouting about all the presents Santa was bringing him. After my declaration that Santa Claus was an imaginary figure, RJ, five, and two years my junior, burst into tears. Tia grabbed her younger brother and tried to console him while screaming at me.

"Why you do that!" Tia tried to cover the mouth of her wailing younger brother. "Stop that cryin' RJ, momma is gonna come out here and we are gonna get in trouble!" I watched the scene develop through the chain link fence separating our yards. Almost on cue, RJ and Tia's mother stormed outside to investigate the cause of her son's distress.

RJ ran to his mother with tears in his eyes and pointed at me.

"She said there wasn't a Santa!" Their mother scooped RJ into her arms.

"Oh RJ, she didn't mean it. She was just joking." RJ's mom said trying to calm her son. She turned to me still standing there watching hand on hip, my face without a hint of remorse.

"You need to apologize right now!" she said authoritatively.

"Why do *I* need to apologize? You are the one lying to your kid." I said in a tone mocking that same authority. Just as RJ and Tia's mom was likely about to remind me of a child's place, my parents appeared and told me to go inside.

Later, Daddy asked why I did what I did. I shrugged and simply responded, "because there is no Santa." All he could do was laugh. That was not the last time my mouth got me in trouble. The way I saw it I was simply following my daddy's advice. "Don't let anybody bully you." He would say. "Stand up for yourself, and if you have to fight, fight."

A true daddy's girl, I loved my father. He had a dark brown complexion, a beard, a booming voice, and stood over six feet tall. He was a teacher and coach and was well liked by all. I always wanted to be with Daddy. Anytime it looked like he was preparing to leave the house, I made sure I looked presentable and had shoes on ready for an invitation to hop in the car and tag along. My daddy made me feel loved and safe. He instilled in me the importance of standing up for myself. He taught me about sports, made sure I learned to swim, and taught me how to ride a bike. Little did I know, those would be my last daddy lessons.

Learning to ride a bike without training wheels was terrifying as a nine-year-old. The tears welled in my eyes as I stood straddling my bike at the top of the hill on my Memphis neighborhood street. The hill's apex was about a dozen feet in front of the steep driveway leading up to the carport attached to our house. The pink and purple streamers swayed gently in the summer breeze as I gripped the handlebars tightly. Up until then, I had only biked the straight parts of the street with the training wheels on. Now they were off, and I was staring down the slope of Applegate street.

"I know you are not about to cry." My dad's voice strong and deep bellowed from above me. A big fan of amusement parks, I too was surprised by my fear. Usually, the bigger the ride and the faster it went, the better. Somehow, riding down this hill brought me to tears.

"I will go too fast. I am scared to fall off." I said shakily. Daddy thumped my thigh.

"Don't be afraid of anything. If you fall, you will get back up and try again. Ready?"

I began paddling while my dad trotted at my side. I approached the downslope, and as my speed picked up and I pulled away from him, he yelled. "Keep pedaling!"

I moved my feet and kept my balance. It felt like I was flying. I laughed giddily as I made it to the end of the street without falling. I rode my bike back to my dad who was laughing and smiling.

"Good job." He said cheerfully. "See, nothing to be afraid of." His warm nature always pushed me to excel, and I believed everything Daddy told me.

I looked for any and every opportunity to be with my father. The times I got the invite to accompany him while he ran errands, I would excitedly hop into the white Daytona with the black rear windshield window louvre and deep burgundy interior and happily strap myself in, thrilled to be along for the ride. Daddy would have talks with me on these drives. On one such drive when I was seven years old, I told my dad I wanted to be a doctor when I grew up. He looked at me and said, "you can do anything you want to do puddin'." Those simple yet powerful words embossed themselves into my mind and would be my guiding light forever.

THE YEAR WAS 1991 AND IT WAS THREE MONTHS AFTER MY TENTH birthday. It was summer break, and the sibling and I were up late watching *Wildcats*. As the screen faded to black and the closing credits began to roll, we heard a house rattling thud from above. The sibling and I exchanged worried glances and quickly trotted up the stairs. Before reaching the top, I slowed my pace and timidly peered through the railing. On the floor of my parents' bedroom was my father. My mother and one of my sisters were frantically trying to get him to his feet. With their help he was able to stand, but he would not stop coughing. I ran to the doorway of the room and stood watching as my daddy continued to cough violently, frothy spit foaming at his lips. With my mother and sister on either side, Daddy walked slowly and shakily to their bathroom. The sibling burst into tears and ran into the room next door. My mother's screams and frantic directives to call 911 filled the entire house. My sister hurriedly dialed the number and with the receiver at her ear she yelled, "It's busy!"

"Keep trying!" my mother wailed.

After a few failed attempts to reach a 911 operator, my mother and sister tried to assist Daddy down the stairs to drive him to the hospital. He was unable to support his weight enough for them to make it down even one step. Back in the room my sister repeated her attempts at connecting to the emergency number and finally got through. She yelled our address in the phone and spoke through sobs as she described the events taking place in our home. Daddy collapsed hard onto the bed. Frozen in place at the room's entrance, tears rushed to my eyes when my mother cried out "Please do not leave me." I watched as my father opened his eyes and looked around at his distraught and panicked family. Then Daddy said the last word I would ever hear him say, "bye." He closed his eyes and I trembled as the collective cries of the Porter family echoed through our home.

It seemed like forever, but finally sirens were audible, and the flashing lights of an ambulance turned onto our street. My sisters and I rushed outside to flag them down and they brought the stretcher through the house and up the stairs. After Daddy and my mother left in the ambulance, my stomach was in knots. The tears had formed large puddles that stung in my eyes and blurred my vision. I had a lump in my throat, yet I could not cry. The trapped cry twisted and pulled at my insides and I felt pressure building in my chest. The room spun and I was overwhelmed by the churning in my belly. I ran to the bathroom, hurriedly pulled down my shorts, and sat on the toilet. Nothing happened. I moaned and pushed. I pushed and moaned, trying desperately to quiet my gut's turmoil, but nothing happened. Then the thought that I was avoiding hit me hard. Daddy said bye. Daddy is not ever coming back. My stomach reacted violently. I glued my bottom to the toilet and grabbed the trashcan beside me. Everything came out then, except the tears.

The next morning, I woke up next to the sibling sleeping beside me. I crept out of bed and went into my parents' room. The room was empty, my parents' bed still in disarray from the events of the night before. I went back to bed and closed my eyes tight, hoping to escape this reality and wake up in a world where my daddy was sleeping in his room. Before I could drift away into an alternate universe, my mother's voice prompted me to open my eyes. Sitting up, I focused on her words.

The knotted sensations returned to my stomach as she spoke.

"Your daddy is gone." She said softly. "He didn't make it through the night."

Following my mother's announcement, my family and I sat in the living room, the television was tuned to BET and music videos played quietly in the background. I stared into space and was unable to focus. I only heard the murmurs of conversation around me. My mind was racing but I was unable to speak. It was as if I had not learned to speak at all. I was also unable to cry. The overpowering grief had turned into body wrenching dry heaves which sent me running to the bathroom in anticipation of projectile emesis. *It's So Hard to Say Goodbye to Yesterday*, a song I had never heard before, started playing softly in the background. The lyrics unleashed the devastation bubbling within me, and I screamed out in pain. The tears found their way out, and I was inconsolable.

My life was forever changed when Daddy died. His absence left a void within me. Even if someone had tried to fill it, they would not have been able to. Following my father's death, I was withdrawn, silent, and angry. I only willingly interacted with Kitt and Frizz, stray cats that I had made a home for. Despite the companionship of my newly found furry friends, the world became a dark place. Kids teased me about my dead daddy. A scrappy girl, I attacked swiftly, pouncing before they finished their taunts. I never backed down to a challenger and would often return home from school with ruined clothing and disheveled hair after tussling with yet another kid. After every verbal or physical explosion, I expected to pay penance, and no matter how steep the price, I would smile inwardly knowing I had stood up for myself just like Daddy taught me.

I WAS SIXTEEN WHEN MY ANGER REACHED ITS BOILING POINT. WHILE working at Discovery Zone, an indoor playground for kids, I was tending to customers at the ticket exchange register when a co-worker hit me with a toy bat.

"Stop it!" I said, before turning to the child in front of me and exchanging her tickets for a stuffed toy. The boy sneered and hit me again. This time instead of a small sting, my legs throbbed. I ended my interaction with the child and turned away from the register. I looked at my legs and they were bruised from the whack of the bat. I winced as I touched the discolored areas on my legs. An indescribable feeling of rage washed over me and the room, once cheery and colorful, took on a red hue. I turned away from the register and could still hear the boy's jeering laughter as I entered the employee only area.

I looked around the room of red fog. It was hot when I picked it up, only the heavy plastic coating on the handle protected my hand from its scorching temperature. I returned to the exchange counter and confronted my assailant furiously swinging my weapon. He yelped when the hot metal landed on his skin and reacted by swinging a fist towards my face. I parried the fist and landed another blow to his arm with the large hot metal tongs and did not stop. My dad's words rang in my mind as I landed blow after blow. The boy stopped fighting, curled himself into his body, and repeated "I'm sorry, I'm so sorry" over and over. I dropped my weapon, put a smile on my face, and returned to my post at the exchange counter register. I was greeting a child making his way to the register when the manager emerged and summoned me into his office. The manager called my mother, and I was fired.

Although the anger would eventually dissipate, and the physical fights would become a thing of the past, "RP", the feisty one, unabashed and unafraid, would always remain alive and well within.

3

FAST AND FURIOUS IN FLORENCE

"Signorina? Excuse me, Miss?" Back in the lobby bar of Hotel Mattei, the bartender's voice startled me away from my thoughts. I looked up and responded with a distracted "Yes?"

"Un altro?" The bartender asked. I looked around and the lively crowd that once occupied the area was gone.

"No grazie, il conto per favore." I responded.

I had revisited every moment of the beginnings of my trip with Kevin and so far, had not come up with a reason for his behavior. I was exhausted and it was late. I hoped Kevin would be sleeping. *Unless those riveting word search puzzles kept him awake*, I snickered to myself as I signed the check.

Entering our room quietly, I breathed a sigh of relief when I found him fast asleep. I crawled into bed and lay beside him. Tomorrow we were going to Florence. Tomorrow would be a better day. Comforted by these thoughts, I closed my eyes and convinced myself that we both just needed to sleep.

The next morning was cordial. At least we were speaking. We made banter at the hotel's continental breakfast and sang along together as we drove to Florence. Marveling over the Italian countryside, I watched as we passed stone homes that seemed to grow out of the lush green hills. As the scenery whizzed by, I thought of how incredible it was that Kevin and I found each other. The combination of commonalities between us from religion to kids and from career goals to sex was rare, and I was both optimistic and hopeful. Kevin was the man who drove from North Carolina in a snowstorm to pick me up in Georgia when my connecting flight was canceled. He was the man who made a long-distance relationship feel not so distanced. This could be the man I would share my life with. I smiled at the thought and caressed his hand.

We arrived in Florence and dropped the car off in a garage in the city center. It was a nice day, cool in the low sixties, and a crisp breeze coursed through the air. The bustling streets were lined with architectural wonders and I marveled at the sight. I loved European architecture. The intricacy of the details, well preserved and beautiful after millennia, left me awestruck. It was my first visit to Florence and the novelty was reinvigorating. We were only in the city for one day and I was thankful for the early start. There was a lot to see.

We located a hop on hop off bus tour stop and waited. The double decker red bus with its logo written in large yellow letters was familiar to me as it turned the corner and approached the stop. The bus arrived and we hopped on. Our adventure in Florence had begun. As an avid TripAdvisor user and having just finished reading Dan Brown's *Inferno*, I was excited to explore Florence. Opening the map that accompanied our tour tickets, I perused the route and its planned stops.

"What do you think?" I said to Kevin, as I pointed to several sites along the route.

"I do not have an opinion." He said coolly, with his gaze fixed straight ahead.

Happily taking the lead, I chose a destination.

"Michelangelo Square it is." I said smiling.

Kevin simply shrugged in response.

"The views of the city are breathtaking!" I exclaimed excitedly as I skipped to the balustrade of Piazzale Michelangelo while taking out my camera. Capturing the panoramic views, I felt light and cheerful. The cool Italian breeze proved pleasant as I admired the square's beautiful flower gardens. A floral display shaped like a heart captured my attention and I strolled over. Looking around for my beau as I approached, Kevin was nowhere to be found. A few flower selfies later, I wandered around taking in the sights and eventually spotted Kevin. I walked over to the Test Drive Firenze demonstration, not at all surprised to find him there. One of my favorite moments was riding along as he drove his self-discovered racetrack, a series of looping Carolina back roads. My gleeful giggles rang out when the velocity pressed my body into the bucket seats of the souped-up Camaro as Kevin sped along the track.

He was speaking with an Italian man dressed in black pants, a black polo shirt, and a black jacket with Test Drive Firenze printed in bold red letters. They were looking at and gesturing towards a gorgeous red Ferrari with black rims. Its gold Ferrari logo was blinding as it reflected the sunlight into my eyes. Kevin was relaxed and smiling. I was excited to see that he was engaged.

"Hey! This is right up your alley!" I said as I approached.

"Yeah, wanna join me?" Kevin asked.

"Sure!" I responded.

After signing waivers and paying for the experience, we were off! Kevin, not a stranger to fast cars, zipped through the Florence streets. The tour guide's unsuccessful attempts to slow him down were hilarious as we charted the GPS set course. He was given the green light to floor it as we approached a tunnel. We zoomed through the tunnel at over one hundred miles per hour, the engine's sounds amplified as they bounced from wall to wall. We were all smiles upon our return to Michelangelo square. He and the guide continued their car banter, while I basked in the afterglow of the adrenaline rush. I hoped this experience was the reset he needed.

Back on the bus, I pulled out the map and shared it with him, energetically pointing out potential next stops. Shrugging in response, he looked around casually and I was again left responsible for navigating our course. We hopped back off the bus in a bustling area not far from what I decided would be our next destination. Marveling over the sculptures at the Loggia dei Lanzi, I eagerly attempted to engage, however Kevin remained cool and distant. The mesmerizing art surrounding me trivialized my relationship woes and I allowed myself to become immersed in my surroundings. I animatedly kept conversation going by discussing *Inferno*. The action takes place in Florence and the sights on our tour served as the setting for some of the books most intriguing plot twists. Kevin only nodded and half smiled in response. His disinterest was palpable. RP's ears twitched. I had not seen this smile before and it was more like a smirk and just like the smile itself; I was confused about how it made me feel.

We approached the Cathedral of Santa Maria del Fiore. As its massive red dome grew larger with each of our steps on the cobblestone streets, so did the distance between us. As I marveled at the beauty of Brunelleschi's design, I fantasized about how I hoped our time together would be. I could almost hear us laughing as we talked animatedly about what to see and where to go next. I imagined kisses in front of cathedrals and on bridges, warm caresses, and subtle public foreplay. A smile formed at the corners of my lips and then quickly faded. There had been no such affection since we left Chicago. While it was still unclear to me where the detour occurred, I was hopeful that we would get back on track.

The placemats on a table outside a café caught my eye and we decided to stop for a bite to eat. *Oh Yes! You're in Florence! Ebbene Sì! Tu'ssei a Firenze!* titled the placemats. They were foot maps with drawings of some of Florence's most popular sites dotted with cartoons of men and women dancing and singing in the city. The placemats contained facts about the renaissance city, like its symbol, il Giglio, and that Florence has seven million tourists annually. He quietly stared at me as I studied the placemat. I looked at him and smiled saying what a cute idea I thought they were. Again, Kevin only nodded in response.

After a beautiful Tuscan meal, eaten in silence, I handed him the map and asked what he wanted to do next. After the Ferrari drive and Kevin's interactions with the guide, I knew the charming man that I had grown fond of was in there and I wanted that person to emerge. Yet again, he shrugged and said nothing. I persisted.

"No really, I want your input."

I could hear the pleading tone in my voice. RP lifted her eyes, scowled, and a hiss escaped from her lips. The tone of my voice was nails on a chalkboard and RP angrily arched her back in response.

"I do not have an agenda. Whatever you want to do is fine." He responded curtly. Each of his statements sounded like a directive for me to stop asking. The smile-smirk reappeared. I tried not to roll my eyes. I needed a drink.

According to Google maps, there was a bar near Ponte Vecchio, another action-packed point of interest in *Inferno*. I decided we would walk the eight to ten minutes from the restaurant to Verrazzano Spumantino al Ponte Vecchio.

Ponte Vecchio was just as I imagined. Several shops were nearby, and I perused the wares in the windows.

"There is a hidden walkway in this bridge!" I exclaimed, speaking aloud more to myself than to my companion. I had traveled solo on numerous occasions and Kevin's silence did not make Florence any less engrossing.

Verrazzano Spumantino al Ponte Vecchio's trendy red décor and black marbled countertops set the tone for a relaxed vibe.

Sipping Chianti and enjoying the atmosphere, I used this as an opportunity to explore Kevin's thoughts.

"Are you enjoying the tour?" I asked.

"Yep." He answered.

"I get the sense there is still tension here." I said in as soft of a tone as I could muster. "What's wrong?"

"Nothing's wrong. I'm fine." Kevin said and the smile smirk reappeared. Annoyed and running out of ideas on how to understand the palpable rift between us, I continued sipping, soothing my aggravation with every taste of wine. The sunset's beautiful colors painted the walls of the bar and I was prompted to check the time.

"Our cooking class starts soon!" I exclaimed. I pulled out the map and placed it on the small, round table. Sharing the address and putting it in Google Maps, I pointed to the general vicinity of the class's location. Without glancing down at the map, Kevin nodded in agreement.

"According to Google, it is less than a fifteen-minute walk from here." I announced.

Again, he only nodded. Motioning for the waiter, Kevin asked for the check. He flipped his card out of his wallet and smacked it against the table. In my wine induced mellow mood, the card hitting the table seemed loud and aggressive. After signing the check, Kevin looked at me intently and said, "It's just the way you say things". Shock joined the sunset orange decorating my face.

"What do you mean? I am using my normal voice, being considerate, and purposefully attempting to be upbeat and keep you included. Can you give me a concrete example of what you are talking about?"

Kevin repeated his unfounded claim without elaboration. The buzz buffered RP's rising anger, and she hissed hazily in discontent. I shook my head incredulously, grabbed the map from the table, and left the bar. I was looking forward to the cooking class more than ever. My eagerness to attend the class was not for the culinary instruction, it was because there would be more wine.

We entered the cooking class space and were seated at a long table with two couples. Still buzzing from the delicious Chianti at Verrazzano Spumantino, RP was contently purring quietly. I immediately noticed several wine bottles in the center of each light grey quartz tabletop and cheered inwardly. The tables had six setups, each equipped with a fork, metal spatula, and a few cups of flour in a neat pile. We sat on the empty barstools and introduced ourselves to the other couples. Smiling faces and warm introductions reciprocated our own. We sipped wine and made small talk with our class companions while waiting for our lesson in Italian cuisine to start. The charismatic man I knew Kevin to be was once again present and accounted for.

The executive chef, Alain Liggia, made his way to the front of the classroom and began his introduction to the pizza and gelato making class. After his opening remarks, we donned aprons decorated with the Florence Food and Wine Academy's logo, a small person encircled by a frame inspecting wine in a glass. The class was fun and informative. Chef Liggia walked us through the dough making process with skill and patience. As a cooking and cookware novice, I found his instructions clear and easy to follow. After the thorough discussion, we separated our flour and added water creating a ball of dough. We were instructed on how to then transform the ball of dough into the base of our pizzas. With the crust prepared we moved on to toppings. There was an assortment of meats, vegetables, and cheeses to choose from. Once we were all satisfied with our creations, we used metal peels to place the pizza into the oven. Getting the pizza onto the peel proved challenging and the laughter in the room demonstrated the challenge was universal. After placing our personal pizzas in the oven, it was on to the gelato. Kevin and I listened intently and worked as a pair during class. We took pictures and laughed together. For the first time since arriving in Italy, we felt connected. I had a nagging feeling it was just secondary to the eyes and ears of others, but I was not going to let that spoil the moment. I was having fun.

"Signora?" Chef Liggia was looking directly at me.

"Yes?" I answered.

"Would you please come and stir for me as I continue my instructions?" Chef Liggia asked.

"Sure." I got off my stool and walked up to the front of the room. Chef Liggia handed me a plastic spatula. He instructed us that the milk and cream mixture needed to be stirred slowly and consistently. I took the spatula and stirred the mixture. Looking into the pot, I became entranced, and a sense of unease washed over me. Chef Liggia continued his lecture on gelato, but his voice now seemed a million miles away.

4

GET OUT THE KITCHEN

"Go on now! You are making me nervous, and I can't stand it! Get out of here girl!" My mother would shriek at me when she noticed I was peering into the kitchen. When I was found out, I would scurry away retreating to the company of Kitt and Frizz. I tried repeatedly to get close enough to learn from my mother as she prepared meals for the family, however her response was always the same.

A great cook and even better at baking, my mother prepared her most elaborate feasts during the holidays. She would wake in the wee hours of the morning on Thanksgiving or Christmas to finish preparing the meal that she likely started the night before. The kitchen countertops would be lined with ham, turkey, spaghetti with meat and cheese, sweet potato casserole, green bean casserole, potato salad, dressing, and dinner rolls. Then there were the desserts: German chocolate cake, sweet potato pies, cheese pies, and pound cake. Year after year, the tradition continued, but anytime I got close enough to witness her culinary prowess, she would yell, "Get out! Get out! Get out!!"

Over the years, I made fewer and fewer attempts to bond with my mother through cooking, and eventually, I stopped trying. The frustration and rejection following my attempts to learn was not worth the skillset. With those deserted attempts, I was disinterested in meal preparation and food became just another necessity. I understood eating was not just for nurturing the body. I understood that in addition to sustaining the here and there of everyday, food enhanced and added nuance to life's journey. While I knew those things to be true, I had grown indifferent to the culinary arts. After leaving the nest, my kitchen contained simple staples consisting of whole grains, vegetables, and breakfast necessities. I stuck to uncomplicated acts in the kitchen and I was content leaving the fancy stuff to the professionals.

I also understood that food was used to express love and that cooking has long been atop the acts of service love language list. Growing up with three older sisters and being up to fifteen years their junior, I learned that for women cooking was often times an unspoken obligation. Having had similar experiences with our mother, my sisters mostly did not learn to cook at home.

"Women are supposed to cook for their men." One of my sisters said to me as I watched her prepare dinner for her husband. I observed the seemingly laborious task of adding this and stirring that. Mostly, I watched my sister. Her movements were swift and jagged, and there was a furrow in her brow. Her body language and facial expressions told a story of anxiety and not one of love. Dinner was done and the man she had cooked for had yet to arrive. My sister and I ate and enjoyed the results of her efforts. The mashed sweet potatoes, green beans, chicken, and corn bread were all seasoned to perfection. The man walked in as I was singing her praises. After changing into sweats, he returned and sat down. My sister went to the kitchen and grabbed the plate she had prepared for him. He took it and with a small thanks began eating. After devouring every bite, he put the plate on the coffee table, my sister picked it up, took it to the kitchen, washed it, and that was that. There were no compliments received or required. Although, I had seen this scenario play out time and again, I did not like it. It felt imbalanced and never translated to a loving interaction. Cooking did not appear to be a loving act of service, but an act of servitude for someone who felt entitled to receive it.

I was in my final year at Vanderbilt School of Medicine and dating Oliver. Oliver and I went to medical school in the same city. After an introduction by mutual friends, Oliver and I started studying together. Our study sessions turned into more frequent hangouts and soon we were inseparable. We went to parties, binge watched TV shows, shared childhood stories, and became the best of friends. He even taught me to fish, but I left the cooking to him. Oliver loved cooking. I was apprehensive the first time he invited me over and made dinner. My skepticism was quickly put to rest when I ate the best pork loin I had ever tasted. His mother and father taught him well.

One night after another spectacular meal, Oliver asked me to cook for him. I responded with lighthearted laughter, not only as a protest, but to remind him that I lacked those skills. It was common knowledge that I did not know how to cook and that I was uncomfortable in the kitchen.

"You know I do not cook." I said still laughing. "Unless all it requires is boiling water or using the microwave, count me out."

"It'll be fun!" Oliver persisted. "I'll get the meat!" He exclaimed sounding way too confident about this entire endeavor.

"OK fine, Ugh!" I said playfully.

On the night of my culinary attempt, my stomach was in knots as I studied the step-by-step instructions. I had pulled up an "easy" recipe for steak and mashed potatoes and had spent hours in the grocery store looking for ingredients and buying the appropriate cookware. Now standing in my Bellevue kitchen apartment, I was anxious and angry with myself for even agreeing to do this. I read the instructions and they seemed simple enough, so I moved forward. You are in medical school; cooking cannot be that hard, right? I thought to myself. I then heard my mother's voice in my mind. "Get out!Get out! Get out!" I shook my head quickly and turned on the stove.

Oliver arrived as I was setting the table for dinner.

"It smells good in here!" he exclaimed as he entered my apartment. I shot him a look that said, "*don't get too excited*" and we both laughed.

I sat across from Oliver, disgusted and embarrassed, staring down at the plate in front of me. My attempt at making steak, mashed potatoes, and broccoli had yielded mediocre results. On the plus side, I was developing my taste for wine and had chosen a nice red for the evening. I was also thankful for the frozen broccoli which I jazzed up with a little cheese. The mashed potatoes were just ok and were a little salty. Then there was the steak, overcooked and rubbery, it was disastrous at best. Oliver tried to indulge me by taking bites of the unfortunate meal, but eventually we both pushed our plates to the side. Sipping wine instead, Oliver joked about the steak.

"I told you I don't cook!" I said dramatically, hoping it was not evident just how embarrassed I really was.

"You are from the south! I expected more from you!" Oliver said playfully. "Didn't your momma teach you how to cook?" My smile faded.

"No. No, she didn't." I stated flatly, trying to muffle her voice once again screaming in my mind. Seeing the distant look that had appeared on my face, Oliver changed the subject.

"Siegfried is huge these days!" He said looking at my white cat with tiger stripes. I immediately smiled and burst into laughter.

"He is the fattest cat ever!" I said with laughter in my voice. As if on cue, Siegfried mewed. I picked up my cat, curled up on the couch, and petted his soft fur.

"You don't care about my cooking, do you?" I cooed.

"That cat looks like he'll eat anything!" Oliver cackled.

We burst into laughter and Siegfried responded with a soft rumble of purrs.

While cooking was not the Achilles heel in my relationship with Oliver, the vulnerability I discovered I had surrounding the act planted seeds of inadequacy. I wondered why preparing a meal was such a big deal. Whether I picked up dinner or had it delivered, a meal was still being shared creating an opportunity to bond over food. Apparently, it only counts if *I* cook it. With feelings of inadequacy leading to anxiety, I became defensive in relationships when the inevitable question "Can you cook?" was asked. Those conversations usually ended with my suitors' shock and disappointment in a southern girl not knowing how to cook. My defensiveness deteriorated these discussions into difficult debates. Like a cat listlessly refusing to learn commands, I decided to no longer entertain the expectation that cooking be a part of my repertoire. It was a chore that I avoided altogether. I shrugged off criticism from friends, family, and suitors and became unbothered by my culinary underachievement. I would learn to cook when I developed a natural curiosity to do so, and until then eating outside my home suited me fine.

Although our romantic relationship ended on a sour note, Oliver and I remained acquainted long after we stopped dating. Years later, while on a trip to D.C., I paid him a visit. During our time spent catching up, Oliver received a package from Blue Apron. He explained that it was a meal kit service he used to explore new recipes. As he unpackaged and stored the items that were inside the box, I looked at the recipe cards. One side of the card displayed the finished and plated product and an ingredient list, and the other side had detailed step by step instructions with photos. I was sold at all ingredients included. After hearing more about Blue Apron, I decided to subscribe. Residency work hours were a thing of the past, as was my anxiety surrounding being in the kitchen. I was ready to invest in learning something new.

Blue Apron made cooking a fun project and was another commonality between me and Kevin, who was also a subscriber. We bonded over food faux pas and delighted in stories of botched efforts. Over time Blue Apron changed our lack of craftsmanship in the kitchen and soon our meals became photo worthy. We kept each other abreast of special recipes and exchanged pictures of our finished entrees. When deciding on activities for our trip to Italy, the cooking class was something that interested us both. We talked about practicing our newfound skills together once we returned to the States. I was proud of the progress I had made. Cooking had created such angst and now I was enjoying myself and learning in the process. Most importantly, I no longer heard my mother's voice in my head screaming, "Get out! Get out! Get out!"

5

GO BIG! GO ROME!

My daze cleared and Chef Liggia's words once again came into focus. He told me my job was done and I received applause and giggles as I gave a tiny curtsy. With the gelato on ice and our pizzas out of the oven, it was time for dinner. We talked amongst ourselves and learned more about our cooking classmates. We were among two couples from the United States and the other couple was from Italy. We touched on a variety of topics from entertainment to healthcare. The conversation was lively and full of laughter. The wine bottles, now scattered around the table, we're all empty. After enjoying our gelato, we each received a certificate of proficiency. The certificates, complete with our names printed on them, had the academy's logo and an il Giglio embossed gold seal along with the signatures of Executive Chef Liggia and the Dean of the Academy, Rosetta Jacopini.

Filing out of the culinary class space and into the cool night air, we were all smiling ear to ear. I tightly wrapped my scarf around my neck and Kevin donned his beanie. I reached for his hand. Kevin took a furtive glance at my outstretched hand, but his hands stayed in his pockets. The snub stung more than the cool air against my face. My feelings were hurt, and I was still in the dark as to what happened between us. A catch rose in my throat and I swallowed it down hard. I had just had the most fun I ever had in a kitchen. I was invited to the front of the class and I happily engaged. I wanted to hold on to that feeling. Focusing on positive thoughts, I shook off the affront and enjoyed our only night in Florence.

———

"We are in Rome! Yay!" I half spoke have sang as we entered the terrace suite of the Grand Hotel Palatino. Prior to leaving Chicago, I upgraded our room in preparation for romance. The accommodations did not disappoint. The bright, yet soft, pastel yellow walls were nicely balanced with deep earth toned bedding and black side chairs. Gold hardware accented the light wood furniture. Double doors led out to the terrace which had a small black metal coffee table set for two. I approached the terrace railing and I looked out at the city. I could not wait to get out there and explore.

I loved Rome and was excited to have an opportunity to return. I had visited years earlier with Joy, my best friend of over twenty years. We toured the Vatican and marveled over Michelangelo's famous masterpiece, the Sistine Chapel ceiling. She and I had a wonderful time exploring the sights of the ancient city. We walked everywhere and immersed ourselves in the culture. We were met with greetings of "Ciao Bella" as we made our way through the bustling city. We took pictures at the Pantheon, the Trevi Fountain, and our favorite, the Colosseum. Several of those photos are framed in my home and I was looking forward to making new memories with Kevin.

I was still gazing out at the city reminiscing and smiling when Kevin joined me on the terrace. I watched him silently as he approached the railing and stood next to me. We had been cordial and respectful. We spoke to each other using words that conveyed common courtesy or did not speak at all. There were no inklings of romance and our once palpable emotional connection seemed nonexistent. We were traveling companions sharing a bed. At least Kevin's eerie smile-smirk had disappeared for now.

We ate breakfast together at Le Spighe, one of the dining halls in the hotel. A beautifully decorated room, white tablecloths covered round tables, four chairs with gold accents at each of them. There was not much conversation during breakfast, which was not surprising. I had decided to make the best of things here in Rome, whether he participated or not. I was on vacation after all and would be back to the daily grind before I knew it. I pulled out my map and charted our course.

The Grand Hotel Palatino, located in the heart of Rome, made getting around a breeze. We were within a twenty-minute walk or a short bus ride to several major attractions. The Colosseum's massive presence was mere steps away. After breakfast, we left the hotel. I happily bopped along towards The Imperial Forums. Since we had plans to go on a Colosseum tour the next day, I chose to walk in the opposite direction. Still sharing the map, I continued to vocalize the next move giving him an opportunity to join in if he liked. We took photos of one another along the way, and although he was just as distant, I was unbothered and peaceful.

After taking photos at the Trevi Fountain, we hopped on a bus and headed to the Borghese gardens. On the terrace in the park, the amazing panoramic view of the city brought a smile to my face as I captured the images. Piazza del Popolo, located directly below us was filled with people. It was a charming and beautiful park. I was disappointed when the romantic scenery failed to ignite a spark between us. We walked in silence back to the bus stop. I pulled out the map and perused the charted course.

"The next bus isn't coming for another fifteen minutes." I

stated breaking the silence. "I am going to walk around and take a few more pictures while we wait."

"Okie dokie." Kevin said and the smile-smirk returned to his face.

I walked away from Kevin and went back into the park. I passed the time taking selfies and making social media posts. Although I wondered what was wrong with Kevin and what that strange smile was about, I did not want to nag him about my perception of his mood. That was a trigger for me, and I was not going to participate in behavior I despised. On my way back to the bus stop, Kevin was talking animatedly to a guy with a red backpack. I was not in earshot of the conversation, but the body language was relaxed and upbeat. Kevin's expressions were engaged, and he listened intently during his exchange with backpack guy. Kevin had again provided imagery to support my concerns. There was something wrong between us. I watched calmly as they continued their interaction until *it* happened. Backpack guy pulled out a map and unfolded it. I could see backpack guy's lips moving and the motions he was making with his hands. Kevin leaned over eagerly and looked at the map. He pointed and made gestures. He was even smiling, the genuine Kevin smile that I had not been the recipient of all day. RP had had enough. The claws were out.

I walked over to the bus stop and looked directly at Kevin as I approached. I glared at him with one eyebrow raised and slightly sucked my front teeth. I walked directly between the budding buds, turned my back to Kevin, and introduced myself to backpack guy.

"The tour buses are running late." Backpack guy informed me.

"Thanks for the information." I smiled weakly. "Kevin, we have city bus tickets too."

I left Kevin and backpack guy and went to check the posted bus schedule. The city bus routes and schedules were confusing, but I was pissed and in no mood to walk. *Fuck it.* I thought to myself when I could not make heads or tails of the route. Whatever bus that came was the one I was getting on. I watched Kevin as he and backpack guy continued their banter. This was the most words I had heard him speak our entire trip. My blood was boiling. A bus pulled up and when the doors opened, I walked to it.

"Is this our bus?" Kevin asked distractedly, still in conversation with backpack guy. I turned to him slowly as I took the first step onto the bus.

"This is the bus I'm getting on." I responded shrilly.

We showed our tickets and made our way to the back of the bus. It was moderately crowded, and I decided to stand.

"What's your problem?" Kevin asked.

While holding onto the railing above me, I cocked my head to the side and stood back on one hip. I looked him directly in his eyes.

"What's *my* problem? *My* problem? *Bruh*! I have been *trying* to engage you this whole *fucking* time. Pulling out maps and asking if you want to do this, or that, or ANYTHING!'" My tone was strong, direct, and sassy. RP was in charge now and I kept going.

"And you know what I got? NOTHING. Not a thing, except for that goofy, fake ass smile."

"Hey, you are getting kinda loud." Kevin said, looking nervously around the bus. I did not lower my voice.

"Oh, that's right. You only care to engage when there are people around. Nah. When I spoke to you like an adult you didn't have anything to say. You told me I was being sassy and had an attitude. Well guess what? *THIS* is what an attitude looks like!" I stared at him like I was seven feet tall and towered over his six-foot two-inch frame. Kevin clinched his teeth. The smile-smirk was replaced with a look of embarrassment and anger.

I took a seat when one became available. I felt better, lighter. RP, never letting disrespectful behavior last long, purred with content after the exchange. I softened after calling Kevin out on his bullshit and wondered if our relationship was salvageable. I wondered if there were a path to reconciliation. There was not much time left in the trip. We had one more day in Rome and then one day in Venice. After that, we would start our journey back to the US. I wondered what would make this trip a better experience and spoke my next thought aloud.

"We could separate." I suggested matter-of-factly. "We are both adults here, and I am completely confident and comfortable continuing the rest of this trip solo." Kevin did not respond.

"I can send you a copy of your Colosseum ticket for the tour tomorrow." I continued.

"I don't want to separate." Kevin said after a long pause.

Everything about his words and actions suggested that he was not enjoying my company. I was confused and wondered silently why he did not take the offer. We got off the bus and found a restaurant and winery near the hotel. We spent the evening at Hysteria La Vacca 'Mbriaca, The Drunken Cow, and tried several different types of wine. Noticing his newly found attempts to engage, I went along, thankful for the ease of conversation.

Drunk with merriment we stumbled back to the hotel and watched passersby from the terrace. The ringing of my phone startled me; people did not usually call when I was away for vacation. I was happy to see that it was Joy and stepped back into the hotel room to take her call.

"Joy!" I squealed her name into the phone. Although it happened often, it was still a surprise that she seemed to call when I needed to hear her voice most.

"Hey love bug!" She answered. "I know you are on vacation with

Kevin, but you have been on my mind heavily. Is everything ok?"

"I must have been sending you a telepathic distress signal!" I laughed and filled her in on the details of the trip.

"Oh wow, I'm sorry boo. Y'all have not even had sex? In Italy?

One of the most romantic places in the world?" As she spoke, her voice raised an octave with every question she asked.

"Exactly. I never expected a complete breakdown in communication, and I *still* do not know what started it. He just keeps saying it is about 'my tone'. Plus, this no sex thing is crazy!"

"Yeah, your big three." She responded.

"Friendship, sex, and the ability to resolve conflict. We are failing on all fronts!" I said with an exaggerated whine.

"No wonder you lost it on the bus!" She joked. We both laughed.

"You sound good though!" Joy remarked, noticing my surprisingly upbeat demeanor.

"I got drunk at the Drunken Cow. I'm great!"

"Girl, go get you some vitamin D." Joy said only half kidding.

"Might as well. I've already blown up at him. Maybe I can get another type of release as well." Joy and I both laughed and said our goodbyes.

Putting down the phone, I looked out onto the terrace. Kevin stood with his back to me, both arms outstretched and leaning on the railing. I could see his muscular back through the striped polo, his dark jeans fitting him to perfection. As I looked at him, I felt the lustful urges within me rise to the surface. The jokes with Joy had become my agenda for the evening. Might as well enjoy this upgrade I said to myself. As I looked around the beautiful room, my lips spread into a devilish grin.

The evening air was cool, yet I stepped back on to the terrace wearing a black cardigan with only skin underneath. I moved towards him slowly and deliberately, like a cat stalking its prey. I removed his right hand from the railing and entered the space between his arms. I returned his hand to the railing beside me and looked him in his eyes with unquestionable intent. Pressing my body and my lips against his, I guided his outstretched hands inward to the bare skin beneath the knit.

I felt his body respond to mine, and soon we were kissing

feverishly. Without a word, he guided me into our suite. The sex was different from the passionate lovemaking just days before back in Chicago. This was two people, having been cooped up together for days, starved for physical affection, ravaging one another. Aggressive and animalistic, the sex left us both spent and satisfied.

Kevin was asleep minutes later. I got out of bed and entered the bathroom. The night's earlier conversation with Joy about "the big three" popped into mind as I turned on the water and ran a bath. Friendship, sex, and the ability to resolve conflict, those were my top desires for a relationship. Sounds simple enough, but the problem was they carried equal weight. Failing in just one category made the whole relationship an *F*. Did Kevin and I have the potential to become best friends? Sure, but could we resolve conflict? That answer looked like a clear no. What about the sex? I entered the soothing water and focused my thoughts on the sex. While the act left me completely satiated physically, I was sure it was not reconciliation. There was no affection afterwards, no gentle goodnight to offset the rough nature of the sex itself. Everything about it was different than any of our prior intimate moments. Kevin was angry. Yes, he gave in to my seduction, but he was angry, and he wanted me to know it. He wanted me to feel it. I crinkled my nose at the thought and before I knew it, a hearty laugh escaped my lips. Reminiscing on past exploits, I soaked in the warm water and let my mind drift away.

6

SEXUAL RECREATION

I was twenty-two years old and in my first year of medical school at Vanderbilt University. Tucked away in an empty classroom on the medical school's campus, I was studying for an upcoming physiology exam when my phone rang. It was Trent, my boyfriend of three years. We met in college and both went on to graduate school in Nashville. After our call, I looked back at my notes, my eyes wet with tears. I wiped them away and suppressed the burning sensation in my chest. A breakup was not something I wanted to focus on. I had a test to prepare for, so, I went back to my work.

Exam day came and went, and grades were posted. My score was only slightly above passing, and that was a sight foreign to me. We were in the student recreational room after a long day of class and I was flipping through my exam, reviewing the wrong answers. I almost did not hear my friend's question.

"How are you feeling?" Nomi asked.

"Girl, that test threw me for a loop. I barely passed and that cannot happen again. I am looking over my answers now." I responded.

"Everybody feels like shit regarding the test. I was referring to your breakup."

I shrugged. "Eh. We had been butting heads for a while about nonsense. It was coming and now it's over, so that's that."

"Do you miss him?" Nomi asked.

"The only thing I miss is consistent sex." I said with a shrug. We both laughed. "No really, I am fine. Thanks Nomi."

Nomi gave me a little nudge. "We can do better than fine! Let's go out this weekend!"

I enthusiastically agreed.

BAR TWENTY3, A TRENDY, NEW CLUB IN THE DEVELOPING Nashville Gulch, was the perfect place to take a break from medical school and unwind. The music was great and the DJ's played all the top hits. The artistic furniture placed at odd angles, made several small dance spaces and there was a large dance floor in the center of the room. We entered the dimly lit venue; the lights gave the room a deep purple hue. I surveyed the crowd as we headed up to the second floor. BarTwenty3 attracted a diverse mix of people. People came to see and be seen. This night was no different and everyone was dressed to impress.

After a few drinks, my friends and I found ourselves dancing while overlooking the balcony railing. Gyrating to the beat, the sexual nature of the rhythmic grinding reminded me of my self-appointed mission for the night. Up until that point, all my sexual experiences had been relational. It was the first time since I started having sex that I did not have a boyfriend and therefore no longer had a sexual partner. After two long term relationships, I wanted sex without the emotional baggage of the relationship rollercoaster. I decided that I would meet someone and fulfill my sexual urges that night. I continued to dance while scanning the crowd.

Perched on the balcony, like a cat high in a tree surveying the world below, my eyes darted through the room. Moments later I saw him. Tall and broad, he maneuvered through the tight crowd effortlessly for a man of his size. I could see from his physique that he worked out, his body appeared muscular in his V-neck sweater and relaxed jeans. I sprang into action.

"I'll be back ladies." I said as I walked away from the group and headed toward the circular staircase. On the ground level dance floor, he was easy to spot. Walking towards each other, he became taller by the second. I bumped into him and placed my hand on his chest to stabilize myself.

"Oh, excuse me!" I said looking into his handsome face. Smiling, I added, "I'm Rosalyn."

He introduced himself and we exchanged numbers.

"What are you doing after this?" He asked.

I smiled inwardly and thought to myself, *Perfect*! It was one in the morning, and I could read between the lines.

"You, hopefully." I stated boldly. He smiled. I turned, walked away, and went back upstairs with my friends. That had been much easier than anticipated.

It was a quarter to three when he arrived at my place. After only minutes of banter, we quickly undressed each other. He looked even better naked than I had imagined, and I admired his body as he got a condom and put it on. He effortlessly lifted me off my feet and I wrapped my legs around him. I was already dripping with excitement from the novelty of the night's events. At the conclusion of our tryst, I lay beside him on the floor of my living room, looking up at the ceiling. *Mission accomplished*, I thought to myself. Feeling sleepy and satisfied, I turned to my guest and told him he needed to leave. The shock on his face was still there as I closed the door to my apartment and headed to bed. Siegfried, a stray kitten I had recently adopted, reappeared now that my guest was gone and leapt into bed with me. We both purred and drifted off to sleep.

Aware of the double sex standard, I knew indulging in my

sexual desires was accompanied by the risk of being labeled a social pariah. Growing up I was told not to be fast, and that casual sex made women whores. I was told boys were bad and the only talks I got about the birds and bees were horror stories of how sex had been the reason for some woman's demise. After popping my casual sex cherry, I did not feel shame or guilt. I did not lose any of my ambition and my dreams were not sloshing around in the toilet. I felt powerful. I felt sexy. I felt in control. By breaking one of society's rules for women: be sexy, but do not have sex, I had unleashed myself from sexual confinement. Indulging in no strings attached sexual pleasure created a sense of empowerment that coursed through my veins. By disregarding societal pressures and the lessons of my youth, I had taken the first steps to gaining complete agency over my sexuality.

I became hedonistic in my pursuits. I was not interested in romance and rejected the falsehood that sex would land me in a black hole of emotion. Sex was simply pleasurable stress relief, and no penis had the superpower to snatch out my heart and leave me in shambles. Following the climactic conclusions, I did not desire to be held. My limited tolerance to petting was catlike, taking only minutes for it to feel unpleasant. I would squirm out of the position of little spoon and writhe away from the arms encircling me. With the deed done and the invitation to my personal space revoked, I would bask in the afterglow in the solace of solitude.

With a deepening understanding of intercourse and mutual pleasure, I began to loathe the notion that the male orgasm was most important. I also rejected the idea that sex was something happening *to* me. I fully expected sex to be a mutually pleasurable experience and was intolerant of partners providing a poor performance. Companions unable to meet my rapidly expanding sexual demands were dismissed, oftentimes during the act itself. My motto was simple, *If I am not going to bust a nut, then neither are you.* The responses of shock and in several cases, anger, from those relieved of their duties was a high. I enjoyed the feeling and would watch straight-faced as they hurled expletives, their male fragility on full display. It was like I was a superhero avenging every woman who had ever told me "the sex was like watching paint dry". My responses to their tirades were metered and calm. "Ok you can go now. No need for anger. Do you want me to walk you out?" I would say blinking innocently, RP's Cheshire cat grin hidden from view. I was not naïve to the potential perils of my behavior. RP kept her claws sharpened and ready just in case.

During a wild night in Atlanta, my friends and I were on a crowded dance floor at MJQ, a hip-hop club. We were there for a Student National Medical Association conference and it was our last night in the city before returning to Nashville. I instantly noticed Spence's babyface, friendly eyes, and great smile, but the cute combo was not enough to pique my sexual interest. However, after dancing the night away at MJQ, Spence and I decided to keep in touch. We developed a friendship over the next year. We were both sports fans and would watch sporting events while chatting on the phone or via messenger. Spence admired my candor. He confided in me regarding life events and often called seeking relationship advice.

I returned to Atlanta for an interview for the residency class of 2011 at Emory University. I called friends in the area and made plans to go out after completing the business end of my short stay in the city. I contacted Spence, who knew of my arrival, and we agreed to watch a game and catch up over a few beers. I teased out the last of my curls just as there was a knock at my hotel suite door. I adjusted my black, knee length, off the shoulder sweater dress, and pulled on some socks as to not ruin my fishnet stockings while lounging around. I opened the door and greeted Spence with a friendly hug. The game was already on the TV in the front room of the suite, and I grabbed a bottle opener for the beer.

We chatted and caught up. Conversation was easy and fun as

always and we both turned to the television when the basketball playoffs got exciting. I glanced at my watch and as 8p.m. was approaching, I decided it was time to end our visit so I could finish getting ready for my evening out.

"This was fun." I said, a genuine smile on my face.

"Yeah it was." He replied, his attention still on the game.

"Ok but it's time for you to go. I have to add some finishing touches before I meet up with my friends."

"Who are you going out with?" He asked.

"My boy Jay and a few of his friends." I replied.

He turned his head to me slowly. "So, you just gonna go out and give some other dude your pussy?"

I burst into a fit of laughter and responded, "First of all, the operative word there is *my* pussy. Second, we don't even get down like that. Breathe into this bag because you are trippin." I said and playfully flung the paper bag the alcohol was in towards him.

He did not return my laughter. His eyes, usually friendly, appeared menacing.

"Alright, I'm going to the bathroom first." Spence got up and left the seating area.

My cat like intuition had me on high alert. I leaped from the couch and moved into the bedroom. I quickly grabbed sweatpants, threw them on under my dress, slipped into my sneakers, and reentered the front room before Spence finished in the bathroom.

Spence emerged from the bathroom a different person. His jaws were clenched, and he lingered in the doorway of the bathroom as he took note of the additions to my ensemble. He pulled the brim of his hat low across his head which obscured the unfriendly look in his eyes. Without words he slowly walked towards me. Closer and closer he approached stopping inches in front of me, the brim of his hat barely brushing against my face.

"Like I said, it's time for you to go." I said sternly. The charming, smiling baby faced man was gone and the clenching of his square jaw was the only noticeable response to my words. His demeanor was meant to intimidate me. My senses tingled and I prepared myself for violence. RP's claws out, my eyes darted through the seating area of the hotel room marking every item I could use as a weapon. I was trembling on the inside, but RP stood tall, one hand at my side, the other resting on the side table at the base of a decorative statue, my first weapon should I need it.

Between me and the doorway, inches from my face, Spence stood there breathing deeply and loudly like a car's engine revving before racing off. A dizzying sense of urgency washed over me.

I looked directly at him, and with a slow and steady growl, I spoke.

"Spence," the pause after his name emphasized the words that followed. "I do not know what your plan is in this moment, but I want you to know, I will fight you to the death. You need to leave."

For what seemed like an eternity, we stood there facing one another, my hand ready to grab the decorative statue at any twitch of his muscles in my direction. Finally, he stirred. Without a word he turned around and exited the room.

I hurried to the door, pushed it closed, and flipped the security lock. I looked through the peephole and watched as he walked away from my room. My knees buckled when he was no longer in sight.

"What the fuck!?" I said breathlessly as I regained my composure and lifted myself from the hotel room floor. I took a deep breath and stepped into the bathroom, removed the sneakers and sweatpants, and replaced them with red thigh high stiletto boots. I added wrist bangles and hoop earrings to my ensemble. As I looked in the mirror to put on red lipstick, I paused and admired the glammed-out woman staring back at me. I thought about Spence and the threats he made with his body language and was proud of myself for displaying strength in that moment. "If they are bigger than you, pick up a brick and knock 'em out." I could hear Daddy's voice loud and clear in my mind. Once again thankful for the conversations with Daddy in his Daytona, I shook off thoughts of Spence, grabbed my clutch, and went out to meet my friends.

By the time I was a young doctor living in Chicago, I oozed sensuality and stood firm in the power of my sex. A passionate and expressive lover, I had become well versed in the love language of physical touch and could use sex to do anything from emphasize a request to diffuse an argument.

Back in Italy, sex was not the solution for the non-argument argument I was inexplicably in with Kevin. The water was getting cold, and I continued to think about my conundrum as I exited the tub. Despite several attempts, Kevin and I had barely communicated since arriving to the country. We finally had sex, more so fucked, and while it satiated my urges, I knew it did not bring us any closer together. Was I to continue this quest for a resolution? Did I still care? I realized the answers to my questions as I climbed into bed. I looked at Kevin, sleeping soundly, and decided I had reached my limits. I was done trying to breach the chasm between us and had quite literally given my last fuck.

7

THESE TEARS AIN'T FOR YOU

As I got out of bed the next morning, my back let me know just how rough the sex was. Yikes! I thought to myself as I stretched, slowly coaxing my sore muscles to life. With barely a glance and a perfunctory "good morning", Kevin got out of bed and entered the bathroom. His demeanor confirmed what I already knew, and with a shrug I readied myself for the day. Braless in a slim fit blue and white striped Polo racerback midi dress, I was slipping into my grey cardigan when Kevin emerged from the bathroom.

"Your headlights are on." He said with that fucking smirk plastered on his face.

I was not amused. *What are we, twelve?* I thought to myself as I stepped into my flat white Vans sneakers. *Could I at least get some coffee first?* I shook my head quickly as my internal dialogue continued. Deciding to say nothing, I looked through Kevin as I walked to the full-length mirror. He was still smirking at me. His facial expression suggested he was awaiting a response to his snarky commentary. Unwilling to participate, I admired my ensemble and gave myself a little wink before gathering my things and heading toward the hotel room door.

"Our Colosseum tour starts soon. I am going to the restaurant downstairs to get breakfast." I stated matter-of-factly and left the room. As the elevator opened on our floor, Kevin had joined me in the hall.

Finishing my coffee, I pulled up directions to the day's destination. Despite my companion's ridiculous verbiage and seemingly purposeful attempts to dampen my mood, I was bubbling with excitement. On my first trip to Rome, Joy and I captured amazing shots of the massive amphitheater from its exterior. We laid down in the grass surrounding the iconic Roman symbol trying to capture the structure in its entirety while animatedly chatting about what gladiator games must have been like. On today's tour, Kevin and I would go inside the arena, and I was amped with anticipation.

Stepping outside, the lively Rione Monti neighborhood streets were bustling with people. Only eight minutes from the Colosseum, I led the way along the Google Maps charted path. I no longer asked if he were interested in helping navigate our course. If he was opposed to the directions I was taking, then he had better say something. Moving along the route, we stopped at Scalinata dei Borgia o Vicus Scelleratus, a partially tunneled staircase leading to the Colosseum, I handed him my phone.

"Take my picture." I said while handing Kevin my phone. My statement was more a directive than a request. Straight-faced and silent, he took the phone.

"Do you want a photo?" I asked as I reviewed the snapshots he took. He nodded and positioned himself under the archway marking the start of the famous staircase. After a few snaps, we continued our silent stroll.

I noticed Kevin brought along his Go-Pro, and I was again reminded of our pre-Italy intimacy. Prior to our arrival, Kevin spoke repeatedly about getting a Go-Pro for our trip. He thought a road trip through the Italian countryside made for a perfect time to test out his new camera. He talked about capturing stills and videos of everything from scenery and structures to sunrises and sunsets. At the start of our journey, he gushed while showing me the device and explaining its features. He planned to set our moments to music and create a video of what was to be the first of many adventures together. With only one day left in the trip, this was the Go-Pro's first appearance.

Arriving at the Colosseum, we joined the tour group and showed our electronic tickets to the guide. During our tour of the amphitheater, I listened intently as the guide discussed its history. With the capacity to hold over 50,000 spectators, I marveled at the architectural feat of the building's year eighty AD construction. I took mental notes when our guide explained the appearance of the holes within the stone walls of the Colosseum. I would later tell Joy that the holes were the aftermath of pilfering. The metals within its stone walls were removed and used for weaponry or other structures when the popularity of the games declined, and the Colosseum fell into disuse. She had wondered about the then mysterious holes on our first visit years ago.

Entering the lower level of the Colosseum, a maze-like array of walls and walkways, the guide shed light on the hypogeum and its use. He described the intricate interworking of motorized ramps that were used to deliver human and animal entertainers to the arena floor above. As we weaved our way through the labyrinth, the guide spoke of events that took place in the historic arena. The small tour group was enthralled by his vivid descriptions of gladiatorial contests, mock sea battles, animal hunts, and executions. I could almost hear the roar of a blood thirsty crowd awaiting a fight to the death.

We left the Colosseum, grabbed a quick bite, and returned to the hotel. Our days in Rome at an end, we gathered our belongings and packed up the car. Kevin placed his Go-Pro on the dash before driving out onto the Roman streets. As we made our way through the city on Via Cavour heading to highway A 24, the sky's colors were changing as sunset approached.The Colosseum was majestic against the streaked polychromatic backdrop. It was beautiful, and the moment felt magical. Although nothing about our trip had been perfect, I was sure he had captured the perfect sunset.

Arriving in Ravenna, we stopped for a bite at Café Mattei. It felt great to stretch my legs after the trip back, and I was also starving. Sitting at one of the many open tables in the sparsely populated space, I glanced at the menu and decided quickly on a pasta dish. After placing our orders, I looked around at the café's décor. The small white tables, appropriate for the limited space, were topped with the usual salt and pepper shakers and napkin dispensers. A transparent casing next to the register contained decadent appearing pastries. Neon signage on the wall behind me caught my attention. The letters, in a cursive purple print read, "Vivere la vita che ami." I pulled out my phone to translate.

"Live the life you love." I said aloud to myself and the words resonated with me strongly. Kevin sat across from me, hands in the pockets of his zipped Nike windbreaker, and only nodded. I used the time waiting for our fare to check my work schedule for the upcoming week. One of my first initiatives as medical director of obstetrics and gynecology, was to fully transition my department to electronic documentation and computerized order entry. Meetings with IT, pharmacy, and nursing administration, along with my usual full clinic and call schedule made for a terribly busy week ahead. Although I had dozed for much of the drive to Ravenna, I suddenly found myself exhausted. After traveling for vacation, I was usually refreshed, with diminished stress levels and replenished mental reserves. In that moment, I knew I would be returning to work no less stressed than I was when I left. I had tried to make the best of my time in Italy, and I did have some fun moments, but this trip was far from the relaxing romantic rendezvous that I had hoped for. My eyes started to water, and I was no longer hungry.

The waitress, petite, with long dark brown hair pulled into a high ponytail, brought out our dinner. Looking up to thank her, she noticed the tears welling up in my eyes.

"Are you okay?" She asked, looking to Kevin and then back to me.

"I am fine, thank you." I responded, touched by her genuine concern.

"Okay." she said with a small smile and left us to our meals.

Feeling overwhelmed, I pushed my food away and towards the center of the table. Placing my elbows on the table in the spot my plate once occupied, I lowered my head into my hands and covered my eyes. The tears that had been collecting came tumbling down and I cried quietly to myself.

I did not cry often. I learned early in life to reserve vulnerability of such magnitude for moments of solitude. I would lick my emotional wounds assuaging my own pain and did not look externally for comfort. If I were to cry in front of others, the tears were either unexpected, or I was in the company of the few I trusted most. The salty droplets trickled down my cheeks, each tear a sweet relief of the tension that had settled in my chest. In those few moments of fragility, I admonished myself for being abroad with an antagonistic partner and mentally prepared for my return to work.

The sound of metal scraping across the floor disrupted my session of self-soothing and I lifted my head slightly. Kevin was scooting his chair closer to mine. He was reaching out to comfort me. Hands still resting on my face, I watched through the spaces between my fingers as the scene unfolded. My tears dried as quickly as they had appeared. I immediately recoiled, incensed by his softened demeanor. The idea that he could be an asshole the entire trip, however now thought I would be receptive to his attempts to comfort me was offensive.

"No, no, no." I repeated in quick succession. My tone was firm, yet at an appropriate decibel level for the subdued space. My reaction stopped his arms from encircling my body, and he put his hands back in his pockets. I took a napkin from the dispenser and wiped my face. I looked at him as my thoughts whirled angrily in my mind. RP's claws were back out.

"You alright?" He asked.

"So." I said. The word a low growl, long and drawn out. "So", said in that manner, was a common prelude to an oncoming verbal onslaught.

"Let me get this right." I spoke slowly at first. My speech quickened with each passing phrase.

"It took *tears* for you to reach out to me and display some sort of affection?" I let the question linger for a moment before I continued. "I have been trying to talk to you like an adult this whole trip, but tears, did it? Really?" I looked directly at Kevin, now sitting beside me, and paused for effect.

He remained mute. Either understanding that my questions did not require answers or unwilling to give any, he just sat there and listened.

"You have been purposely withholding affection this whole time? For what? *Punishment?*" My rolling eyes emphasized the annoyed hostility in my voice. "Were you *waiting* for me to cry? Was I supposed to cry five days ago? Would that have persuaded you to not be a dick the entire time?" Again, I did not expect an answer. It seemed that by displaying my ultimate form of vulnerability, I had stumbled upon the master key to his affection and my tears made me worthy of his touch. My rage was incited further. With a raised brow, I continued. "Since you are oh so concerned about my emotional state all of a sudden, I'll gladly fill you in on the reason for my tears."

I ranted on and described the hectic schedule I reviewed minutes earlier in painstaking detail. I also included that the vacation had not been relaxing which marred my plan to tackle the first weeks in my new role feeling bright eyed and refreshed. "And after all of that, you still can't clarify for me what the problem was in the first place!" I finished my diatribe and picked up the napkin rolled silverware.

"Sorry I ruined your trip." He said, sarcasm dripping from his words.

"Thanks for your bullshit sentimentality, but I'm good without it." I said with a neck roll that ensured my *sassiness* was apparent. "These tears ain't for you." Suddenly ravenous, I pulled my plate back to me and devoured my meal.

8

LOST AND FOUND IN VENICE

Our journey to Venice started early the next morning. My night had been a sleepless one, and my mood; sedated. I was calm, comfortable, and completely divested from the trip's relational component. It was a little after sunrise when we packed up the car and left Ravenna. I typed directions into the GPS and started the soundtrack for the drive.

In the planning phase and prior to our arrival in Italy, we had decided to return the car first. Our return trip to America started at four in the morning on a Sunday. Returning the car would be one less thing to deal with and obtaining public transit to the airport seemed simple enough. After settling with the rental agency, we gathered our luggage, exited the airport, and started walking to the Alilaguna. Ten minutes into our hike to the shuttle boat dock, I was hot and sticky. My luggage, an orange and black quilted patterned suitcase, was outdated, and I was kicking myself for not having upgraded travel gear. Having only two wheels made maneuvering the medium sized suitcase and personal item along the uneven streets a challenge. My suitcase and I were both dragging when the ferry dock finally came into view and the sight gave me renewed energy.

Another ten minutes later, we reached the docks. The line to the ticket counter was annoyingly long. *At least we were standing still*, I thought as I looked up which ferry to take on the hotel's website. The line moved slowly, and my mood deteriorated with each passing minute. At long last, it was our turn at the booth, and we bought tickets for Liniea Arancio. Cautiously stepping along the slippery ramps, we got on the ferry and gave our bags to the attendants.

"What the fuck." I breathed aloud to no one as I slouched into a window seat on the ferry, relieved to be rid of my bags. I relaxed my body and leaned my head against the window. The packed and bumpy forty-minute boat ride into Venice did not aid my increasingly aching muscles or my mood. Looking out I noticed the city approaching, its multicolored houses decorated the canal. We exited the shuttle at Guglie and lugged our bags to a water taxi stop. Twenty minutes later, the water taxi was dropping us off on Cannaregio Canal directly in front of Carnival Palace.

The hotel's unassuming red brick exterior with its name in simple font centered above the door was in stark contrast to its decadent interior. Entering the lobby through automatic glass doors each decorated with a Venetian mask, we were greeted by friendly staff. The sleek black reception desk was topped with white marble and the impeccably dressed host checked us in efficiently. The bellhop took our luggage, and we were shown to our room.

The plush, luxury terrace suite of the Carnival Palace in Venice, the room that was to be the grand finale of our amorous adventure, was breathtaking. The pictures online paled in comparison to what was before me. The room was a work of art. Its walls were papered in glamorous off-white baroque, the perfect backdrop for the gorgeous furnishings. The bed's venetian white pillow top headboard was carved and glinted with silver accents. The bedding was white and fluffy, decorated with a pale lavender duvet that shimmered in the light. The bathroom, covered in venetian marble, offered a walk-in shower complete with customizable mood lighting. Double doors led to a study containing a white writing table and bench, as well as a chaise lounge in the duvet's iridescent lavender. Accessing the terrace from the study, fantastic views of Venice could be seen in either direction. The walls of the private balcony were high and created a romantic space for the outdoor jacuzzi tub.

Taking in each glorious detail only amplified my tired and cranky disposition. RP's claws were out again, but this time her anger was directed inwardly. Instead of being inspired by my surroundings, I was reminded of the fluttering flights of fantasy I had when booking the place. The room's opulence and private balcony jacuzzi coupled with the charm of Venice was supposed to end our trip with an exclamation point. I now rolled my eyes at those thoughts and hopped in the shower. Hoping to reset my disposition, I turned on the purple mood lighting for good measure. Having washed the morning away, I felt better, at least I was no longer angry. I put on a taupe knee length sweater dress, tights, and tall brown boots. I wrapped a cream scarf around my neck and waited outside on the terrace for Kevin to get ready. I looked out at the canals and bridges crisscrossing through the city. I watched as people got onto gondolas and rode away to their destinations. When Kevin was ready to leave, we left the room to explore the last stop on our vacation.

St. Mark's square was a thirty-minute walk from Carnival Palace, and our private canal tour did not start for several hours. I suggested we walk so we could sightsee along our route. Kevin nodded in agreement. We strolled along the cobblestone streets at a leisurely pace. It was a beautiful day. My mood had brightened, and my self-critical thoughts seemed miles away. I allowed myself to become immersed in the world around me. I took pictures and enjoyed the architecture of the buildings. The streets were lined with gift shops. Most window displays contained elaborately decorated venetian masks. The Venetian Carnival was an event I hoped to someday experience. In one window, a statue of a unicorn, reared up on its hind legs, caught my attention. My longest and best friend, Chris, started calling me his unicorn years before. Forged in middle school, our long-term platonic friendship spanned over twenty years. Growing up, Chris was my neighbor, classmate, fellow band member, and we both ran track. We supported each other through countless life challenges and our friendship thrived despite relationship status changes and distance. Remembering a wild weekend in Houston, I giggled as I recounted being the only female in an otherwise all male crew earning myself the nickname, "The Unicorn". The mythical creature seemed out of place in the window display alongside carnival masks, jewels, and handblown glassware. It was as if it had been put there just for me, and I smiled as I snapped a photo.

It was a bustling Saturday in Venice. People filled every cobblestoned walkway of the maze-like city. Along our walk, several people approached us forcibly peddling their wares. I politely declined, a firm "No, thank you" and a shake of my head was enough to allow continued passage down the street. Kevin treated the street vendors like the scam artists he believed them to be, with a forceful "nope" while aggressively brushing past them. I noticed that I was not surprised by his behavior, it was only shocking that it was directed towards someone other than me.

Continuing along our route, I took more pictures as we passed the Rialto Bridge. The GPS was spotty. The proximity of the winding Venice streets to one another challenged the technology. The scent of food disrupted our navigational problems and we stopped to eat. After perusing the menu, I picked up the wine list, which garnered my companion's attention.

"Drinking already, eh?" Kevin said with a smirk and lifted eyebrows.

"Yep." I replied with a smile that said, fuck you.

"Since I drive you to drink, maybe you should go on the tour on your own." Kevin offered.

"My drinking and your accompaniment are not mutually inclusive, however if you would like to excuse yourself from my presence, feel free." I said straight-faced and blinking at him repeatedly. My fluttering lashes made the use of expletives unnecessary.

"Yeah, I think you would enjoy the day better without me around. I will get something to eat at the hotel." Kevin got up to leave, looking to me before walking away. Relieved by his decision, I had already turned my attention back to the wine list.

After finishing my delectable meal of risotto al nero di sepia, risotto cooked with cuttlefish ink, paired with a Masi red blend, I pulled out my phone and studied a map of the area. I was close to the meeting place for the canal tour and with an hour before I had to be there, I paid the bill and was on my way. After the expected ten-minute walk turned into fifteen and I still did not appear closer to my target, I suspected a misstep in navigation. I retraced my steps, gained confidence in my position, and then rerouted the course. The meeting time for the canal tour was now quickly approaching.

Half past the deadline, I finally made it to St. Mark's square. Since I had missed the tour, I decided to walk around instead. RP was hissing at me again, but I ignored her for now. I wanted to enjoy the little amount of time I had in Venice and would deal with the self-criticism later. St Mark's square was a lively space. I visited the Basilica San Marco and Doge's Palace, taking pictures and reading about their histories on my phone. Hours later, I headed back towards Rialto Bridge. I stopped at Osteria, a wine and coffee bar overlooking the Grand Canal. Taking a seat at a table on the patio, I looked out at the water. The late afternoon sky was cloudy, and the air had a mild chill. As the waiter approached, he turned on a patio heater nearby. The waiter took my order and offered me a blanket, and I was happy to have happened upon such an accommodating establishment.

Sipping wine with a warm blanket on my lap, I observed the boats passing by and wondered if either of them was the one I missed. Couples getting on gondolas, looking lovingly into each other's eyes captured my attention and RP's hissing was loud and clear. I resented my choice to take this trip with Kevin and wondered if there were signs that would have alluded to his inability to communicate. Was there something I missed that spoke to our incompatibility? Having spent my childhood and adolescence walking on eggshells, I became keenly attuned to the emotional state of other people. I watched and learned more about those around me through observation than the words they said. I also sensed things and oftentimes felt ill intentions before outward displays of hostility. I had grown to take pride in my skill of perception.

So, what did I miss? I knew we did not know everything about one another, but we had both been a part of each other's worlds and growing together seemed plausible. I met his friends and coworkers and he met a few of mine. We talked about his active duty in the military and his mental health. We discussed family and life stressors. I teased him when I opened his cabinets and got *Sleeping with the Enemy* vibes, everything in its appropriate place and labels to the front. He clearly had OCD, but that was not a dealbreaker. We wanted the same type of life and for a while, we felt good together. Unable to reveal the missing piece, and RP satisfied with my mental search, I let it go and enjoyed the view and the wine.

The sun was setting by the time I finished my libations. An early morning ahead, I decided to make my way back to Carnival Palace. Although GPS had proved to be useless, it was the only navigational tool at my disposal, and I charted the course to the hotel. Once again, a straight shot, this time in the opposite direction lit up my screen. Phone in hand, I followed the route. Simultaneously following the route and looking for street signs and landmarks, I ran into dead end after dead end. My GPS rerouted again and again, and I was lost in a sea of buildings.

Walking along yet another narrow canal lined street, I noticed excited murmurs in the distance. The voices grew louder with each step I took. Looking up and around then back to my phone, I was about to take one more step when the words became intelligible.

"Signora! Signora! Attento!" A chorus of voices saying, "Miss! Miss! Careful!"

I considered the translation and immediately stopped in my tracks. Looking up, I found myself on a street ending at an embankment and one more step would have landed me in the canal.

"Grazie!" I yelled back to the men across the water. Turning around again, I could feel myself becoming frustrated and my thoughts became harder to still. I walked in the general direction of the blue line eagerly searching for anything that looked familiar. The streets grew quiet, and everything appeared alien as night crept upon the city. I was lost in Venice. I was alone in Venice. I had traveled sans company on several occasions, but to be on a trip with someone and still feel alone reminded me of a time and place I had no desire to return to. I sighed audibly and was just about to rework my strategy when I saw it. There, in one of the store windows was the unicorn, reared up on its hind legs, seemingly out of place, surrounded by masks, jewels, and handblown glassware. Relief wafted over me. Pulling up my photo gallery and using the store as a starting point, I followed my pictures like breadcrumbs back to the hotel.

It was dark when I entered our suite. Happy my bags were in the study; I opened the double doors and prepared my belongings for the journey home. Showered and prepped for the following day, I made the chaise my bed for the evening. Only one thought filled my mind as I fluffed the pillow and settled into the comfortable oversized chair. Tomorrow I was returning home to my West Loop condo in Chicago, back to Sox and Scrappy, and to the sweet relief of solitude. A smile spread across my lips as I drifted off to sleep.

LIVELY LONER

"Congratulations!" Nomi said enthusiastically as we ate our lunch outside at one of the benches of the medical school campus.

I did a little celebratory raise the roof and said, "Thanks girl!" I had just been elected social chair by the medical school class and was now a member of the student government body. "I think I know how to throw a good party; I went to college in New Orleans!" I continued. Being elected social chair did not come as a surprise. In the few months since starting medical school, I had met the entire 105-person class.

After acceptance letters were sent, prospective students received an invitation to second look weekend. It was an introduction to Vanderbilt Medical School, its faculty, and its students. The weekend was filled with information. During the day we toured the campus and learned about classes and how they were structured. Vanderbilt was my number one choice and having already accepted the invitation to join the class of 2007, I drank in all the details. In the evenings, students attending the school took us around the town. At the off-campus gatherings, I chatted with as many of my would-be classmates as I could. I found the diverse group, hailing from various walks of life, friendly and interesting. I was fascinated by the stories they told. By the end of the weekend, there were several confirmed attendees and on the first day of class I already knew eighty percent of the room by name.

During the first few weeks of class, I sat next to a person I had not met yet and made new acquaintances daily. I had always been curious about people. As a young girl, I would sneak around, peering through the railings of the staircase in my home, watching my older sisters' interacting with friends and dates, looking for a moment to insert myself in grown folk's business. I would watch and listen, stealthily picking up details about topics well beyond my age. I was inquisitive and hurled question after question at their guests. Eventually, I would become bored with their tales and would wander off to entertain myself. The stories I created in my mind proved more exciting than their realities.

After two years in the position, social chair merited me the moniker, "Rosalyn, I bring the party to you." There were celebrations for everything from the end of exams to holidays. I believed letting loose was the key to happiness and enjoyed watching revelers drop the weights of medical school and lift their spirits. Double fisting champagne bottles as I moved through the crowd, I would greet guests and fill glasses with one bottle, the other reserved for my personal use. I would make sure the music was fun and energetic, ready to request a different song or jump in and pull people onto the dance floor if there were to be a lull. Outgoing, outspoken, and outlandish, I became the go-to master of ceremonies for any event an organization I was a member of hosted.

It was early 2005, weeks after the devastating Indian Ocean tsunami, and I was emceeing a tsunami relief date auction. Entering the venue hours before it would start, my mental headspace preoccupied, I reminded myself of the job at hand. We must be the personality today. RP reminded me. Bring the party. After my internal dialogue, I reviewed the lineup, music, and my own choreography. I would be auctioned off last, and the song I chose was *Bootylicious* by Destiny's Child. I greeted the participants and we prepared for the show.

There was an excellent turnout, marketing the event on both Meharry Medical College and Vanderbilt's campuses, the attendees were a diverse mix. Perfect! I thought to myself and walked on stage to start the event. I owned my role and took liberties with the scripts given to me appealing to the crowd as I described daters. Energetic and spirited, the crowd actively participated cheering and screaming wildly when the daters took the stage. The show was firing on all cylinders and I was announcing a brief intermission when Oliver walked in.

Our romantic involvement had ended suddenly. The abrupt shift from inseparable to radio silence had hurt and seeing him brought on a fresh wave of emotion. Months before the date auction, Oliver suffered a personal tragedy that I was all too familiar with. I was with him when he got the phone call about the death of his father. I contacted his closest friends and we all stayed with him until he wanted to be alone. During the days that followed, I assisted in any way I could, and accompanied him to his father's funeral. After the services, he stayed with family and I returned to Nashville. Weeks went by. At first, I called frequently to check on his condition. After I received no answers, I stopped calling. One day he popped up on messenger, and I sent a message.

How are you feeling?

There was no response. He either logged off or went incognito. I would later learn through the grapevine that there was someone new.

I stepped off the stage after announcing the scheduled break in the show and was greeted with "good job" from several members in the audience. I was happy to know they were having a good time. I thanked the winners of date bids for their contributions and as I was walking to the bar, Oliver and I locked eyes. He and the someone new were heading in my direction.

"Hey!" He greeted me with enthusiasm and introduced me to his date, Kendall.

Maintaining my emcee mask of the evening, I stayed in character.

Plastering on a smile, I responded.

"Hey you! Hey Kendall! Nice to meet you! Thank you both for coming!"

Sauntering away before they could reply, I made my way through the sea of partygoers and got a drink. I was aware of my reaction to seeing Oliver for the first time since his father's funeral. The disrespect of premiering his relationship status change at my event left my chest stinging and was impossible to ignore. The show must go on. I said to myself before walking back out onto the stage. By the time it was my turn to be auctioned, I had still not gotten used to Oliver's and Kendall's faces in the crowd. I suppressed my feelings as *Bootylicious* started to blare from the speakers. Ending my dance with a mic drop and walking my bid date to the back of the bar, I picked up another mic and thanked the crowd for their donations and for having such amazing energy. Encouraging them to keep it going, I turned the party over to the DJ. Watching the room bursting with energy, I felt accomplished and was satisfied with a job well done.

Although I had several friends and even more acquaintances with whom to party the night away or with whom to discuss Oliver's offenses, I stealthily disappeared from the event. With the trigger of abandonment hot wiring my emotional state, I needed to find peace and longed for the seclusion of my home. Early in life, I learned that only I could tend to the pain of internal injuries. I learned that my hurt was mine alone, people could not fix what they did not feel and likely would not try. I retreated to my safe place to lick my wounds. I would never seek an explanation for Oliver's cessation of communication or the dissolution of our relationship. My life had taught me that people's emotions were volatile, and anyone could cast you aside at a moment's notice. One day I would tell the tale of Oliver and Kendall to my closest friends. By then, with my wounds healed, the experience with Oliver is just another story.

AFTER MY FATHER'S DEATH, I CRIED INCESSANTLY. MY SOBS WOULD spiral into dry heaves sending me running to the bathroom but there was nothing left inside. I was not eating. I was not sleeping. The air was thick and some days it was hard to breathe. The loud, laughing, little girl was tucked away deep inside. I could feel the emotional weight of my family and the grief of those around me amplified my own. I could hear their cries through heavy hearted attempts to carry on with life. I became withdrawn and self-contained and was disinterested in people and their attempts to engage. I isolated myself in my room, and like a cat in a box, I felt safe there. In my room, I was relieved of the burden of external hurt. My own heartache was unbearable.

After Daddy died, my mother came into my room and started packing some of my things. Not talking much, I only watched as she placed several outfits, underwear, and shoes into a bag.

"Let's go". She commanded.

I grabbed my journal before following my mother out of the house and into the blue minivan. Tears streamed silently down my face as I remembered the family road trips with Daddy in the driver's seat of the blue van. I noticed my mother watching me in the rearview mirror, wiped my face, and laid down on the seat. As we approached a familiar building, I sat up and looked at my mother questioningly.

"You are going to stay with Vonnie and her mother for a

while." She said, and then mumbled something under her breath that sounded like, "I can't deal with you."

My stomach churned and I felt tears well up in my eyes again. I quickly wiped them away before they slid down my cheeks.

Vonnie was one of my childhood friends. Her mother, Mrs. Retop, a teacher at the elementary school I was now leaving, was my favorite. My mother had decided we were moving to Germantown and I would attend my new neighborhood's school. Mrs. Retop greeted us as we pulled into the driveway. She came around to my door and opened it.

"Go on inside, Vonnie is in her room". I grabbed my journal and my backpack. I got out of the van slowly, and before going inside I looked back at my mother with the same questioning look.

"Go on now." My mother said to me. I turned and went inside.

I sat down on the sofa and took in my surroundings. I had been to the Retop's home on several occasions, yet I felt like a stranger in a strange land. My times with Vonnie were always fun, but this visit was different. I did not want to play. I did not want to listen to Mrs. Retop and Vonnie's perky voices. I was grieving and living in a world of loss and had now been cast out of my home. I was confused by my presence there. I sat and stared off into the distance wondering why I had been sent away and for how long. Mrs. Retop's voice garnered my attention.

"Don't you want to go upstairs with Vonnie? I know she has been wanting to see you."

I did not want to go upstairs with Vonnie. I wanted to go home. I looked at Mrs. Retop and tears came spilling down my face. I curled up on the couch and sobbed silently.

"You are going to stay with us until you feel better." Mrs. Retop explained in a soft voice. "Getting away from the house where it happened will be good for you."

I cried harder in response and soon I was back in the bathroom, vomiting what was not there. I washed my face and rinsed the taste of bile from my mouth. I looked at myself in the mirror. The sooner I appeared to be better; the sooner I could go home. With tears continuing to stream down my face, I used my fingers to stretch my mouth into a huge grin. I studied my reflection. My eyes were red with tears. My hair was in loose, old ponytails, and my clothes which had loosened over the last week sagged. I wanted to cry as I stared at the fatherless child that stared back at me. Instead, I pried my lips apart into a wider smile. The more the tears stung, the broader I smiled. In that moment, Rosalyn was tucked away, and RP was born. RP would speak when I had no words. RP would play when I just wanted to be left alone. RP would protect me. Mrs. Retop knocked on the bathroom door. "Rosalyn, are you ok in there, sweetie?" RP smiled brightly and I wiped my eyes.

"Yes ma'am." RP responded with a hint of cheerfulness in her voice. RP would give them the show they wanted.

Day after day, I was coddled and coaxed. I acted and appeared lively and feigned well-adjusted child while the duo desperately tried everything to nurse me out of my sadness. Vonnie and I played video games and we watched movies. I even let their two white Shih Tzus lick me, which grossed me out. I learned how to live the duality my zodiac sign suggests, wearing a smiling face that concealed my grief. I learned to be interactive and introspective simultaneously. Engaging in a living performance while preoccupied with my own thoughts, I hovered over myself, watching as RP and Vonnie played together while I wrote in my mental journal and tended to my emotional wounds.

I was there for weeks. I wondered if I would ever convince my hosts that I was feeling better. One day my mother appeared, and I got to go home. When my mom picked me up to take me home, it was not to the home I remembered. We had moved to the suburbs. Moved away from Tia and RJ. Moved away from the memories I had with Daddy. My adult sisters were gone, and of the two youngest children, my mandatory stay with the Retop's let me know I was not the favorite. Entering the new home, bigger, but with a similar layout to the other, I was relieved to see my cats. Away from everything and everyone I knew and having completed my sentence of forced play; I was finally alone.

As I got older, I continued to have a selective interest in people and RP remained my protector. Most of my curiosities continued to lie inward, and the deeper understanding of self was important to me. Although well acquainted with all 105 medical school classmates, I remained fiercely protective of my personal space, and kept only a small group of close friends. I loved my role as social chair and took pride in being the life of the party. However, it was a job, and I was drained by the interchanges. Being alone allowed me to review, reflect, and recharge. Being alone was my safe place and became my favorite pastime.

10

THE JOURNEY HOME

My phone's alarm startled me awake, snatching me away from a dream of solitude and *Fallout 4*. I jolted and found myself sprawled on the luxurious lavender lounge chair in the study of the Venetian terrace suite. The five hours of sleep passed quickly, and I was exhausted, my labyrinthine adventure in Venezia proved more tiresome than I thought. With a quick little whine, I turned on the side table lamp. I was then overtaken by excitement. We are going home today! That thought was the second wind I needed. I got off the couch and prepared for travel.

Shuffling outside the double doors leading to the study let me know that Kevin was also awake. Opening the doors, I observed that he was packed and ready to go. After a sweep of the room for any unpacked items, we headed down to the lobby.

"Very early start for you two." The receptionist stated as we approached the desk to checkout.

"Yes." I spoke. "Very early." I gave the receptionist our room number and we completed the checkout process. "Are the water taxis available now?" I asked while signing the last of the receipts. Looking out the lobby's glass doors, the Venice streets were dark and quiet. The water taxi stop in front of Carnival Palace was unattended.

"Oh. No. Not at this hour." The receptionist stated plainly.

It was just approaching four in the morning. With holes now apparent in our meticulous planning, I considered why we did not make concrete accommodations for our return trip. *Maybe, it was because we thought we would converse on the trip and have plenty of time to iron out that one final detail. This was a prime example of why the ability to resolve conflict is a part of my big three.* I crossed and uncrossed my eyes. Internal dialogue concluded, I looked back to the hotel staff person.

"What would be the best way to travel to Marco Polo Airport at this hour?" I asked.

"You will have to walk to Piazzale Roma. There you will find the buses and maybe private taxis."

"Can you give us directions? I don't trust the GPS on my phone right now." I said and snickered thinking of how helpful it had been the night before.

"Of course." He said and then removed a map from a drawer, opened it, and placed it on the marbled countertop. Turning the map to me he grabbed a highlighter and started his instructions.

"Leaving out of the hotel, you will turn left. You will then cross this bridge."

He highlighted Ponte dei Tri Archi before resuming instructions for the route that entailed crossing a second longer bridge before reaching the transit station. He handed me the map with its bright yellow markings. I thanked him and grabbed my luggage. The automatic glass doors opened as we approached, and I looked back briefly to adjust my bags. As I ensured my personal item and mid-size were strapped tightly together, I caught a glimpse of the hotel desk attendant's face, and in that moment, I knew our route to the transit station would not be as simple as highlights on a map.

Leaving Carnival Palace behind and turning left on Fondamenta Cannaregio, streetlights brightened the path as we made our way to the transit station. Although warmer than the day before, it was still cool, and there was a thick mist in the air. My bags were cumbersome and jostled behind me on the uneven cobblestone streets. I was thankful the steps of Ponte dei Tri Archi were shallow, as I pulled the bags across. The mist morphed into a drizzle as we approached the second bridge.

    The Ponte degli Scalzi, a stone walking bridge across Venice's Grand Canal, was beautiful in the dark, its lights gave it an ethereal glow. As we approached the crossing to one of the longer bridges in Venice, made up of over one hundred steps, I paused to switch arms and dry my luggage handle that had become slick in the rain. Kevin paused when I did. We had not spoken since parting ways the day before. Having righted myself, I grabbed the handle and lugged my bags across the bridge.

    Reaching the other side, my curly hair plastered to my face, and my face wet with a mixture of rain and sweat, my arms cried out from the strain. Our twenty-minute walk was coming to an end and the Piazzale Roma was finally in view. The closer we got to the transit station, more travelers joined us along the route. It was almost 4:30 a.m., and although the area was not densely populated, I was surprised by the number of people traveling at this hour.

    I wrestled with my bags as we walked atop white and yellow checkered pattern lines signifying our entry into the transit space. There were buses lined up diagonally beside one another, but most of their lights were dimmed. Only a single driver was visible standing on the outside of one of the buses. I looked around for taxis. There were only two other vehicles in the lot, and since both lacked signage, neither was an obvious taxi.

    "Heavy bags, yeah?" A guy said as he passed, also adjusting his luggage.

    "OMG!" I responded with a pained laugh.

    Kevin, a few steps ahead of me, looked back.

"Need some help?" Kevin smirked.

I only glared at him in response and kept walking. I thought my look stated the obvious and was shocked when still smirking he asked again.

"Need some help?"

"With what Kevin?" I asked. I was annoyed. "We are here now. If you had the physical reserves to assist me in getting here, you could have offered to help much earlier."

"You could have asked." He snapped.

I looked at him and with RP's growl in my voice, I said, "I would rather drag this fifty-pound suitcase up and down every step in Venice than to ask someone for help offering it only to keep from being ill perceived by others."

Overhearing "driver holiday" and "finding another way" from a couple several feet away, I diverted my attention away from Kevin.

"Did you hear that?" I asked absentmindedly as I walked toward the voices.

I introduced myself as Kevin and I approached the couple. Their body language suggested high stress levels and they appeared to be looking for a solution to a problem. After a brief conversation, we all found ourselves in the same boat. It was a driver holiday in Venice. Busses were running on a more limited schedule and not many private taxis were available either. The five o'clock bus we were all hoping to board would not be running that day.

A little after 5:00 a.m., the transit station was filling with people, and more bus drivers were visible. The first bus would not leave for another forty minutes and that would put us at risk for missing our flight. We were contemplating options when I noticed another unmarked car pulling into Piazzale Roma. The car circled slowly as if the driver were looking for someone. As the car pulled nearer, I inspected it and its driver and although I did not initially see any signs, I knew it was a taxi.

"That's a taxi," I said to the group as I ran toward the slowly moving vehicle. The driver rolled down the passenger side front window. His driver ID dangling from the rear-view mirror confirmed my hunch.

We did not bother haggling with the price. All of us knew the one hundred euro fare was exorbitant, but we split the cost and after figuring out how to get all our bags in the car, we jumped in. It was a tight space. One person sat in the front and Kevin and I squeezed in the back with the other person and her carry-on bag. Cramped on the back seat of the taxi was the closest we had been since our anger bang in Rome. I shook my head at the deterioration of our relationship. With the transportation problem solved; I was reminded of his lame duck offer to help with my bags. I rolled my eyes. I had lived alone for over a decade and had traveled alone for years. Doing for myself, by myself, was what I knew and what I did. As the driver pulled out of Piazzale Roma, I checked my watch and let out a sigh of relief. We were going to make our flight.

After a short two-hour flight, we had a four-hour layover in Amsterdam. Our journey home was smoothing out and the smell of coffee lured me into one of the restaurants in Schiphol International Airport. Feeling light and airy, I reminisced about my previous visits to Amsterdam. The most recent time was less than a year before and thinking about that trip I took with my girls made me giggle to myself.

Kevin was sitting across from me watching me intently. He had the look of a man about to speak. Curious, I perked up my ears. He started by shaking his head.

"The way you say things." One of his catchphrases of the trip was back.

"Tell me more." I spoke, leaning forward with exaggerated interest.

"Like at the hotel this morning. The way you took control." He spewed.

"So, you are angry that I took control of checking out of a room I reserved?" I tilted my head and squinted my eyes. "Or was it getting the directions?" I paused. His comments were insensible.

"You could have jumped in at any moment." I stated. When Kevin did not speak, I did. "My having a voice should not make you feel diminished. I am not going to quiet myself so you can 'be a man'." I used air quotes. I shrugged and added, "We would still be in Venice if it were not for this control you speak of." Kevin did not respond, and we finished our breakfast in silence.

The sun beamed through the large windows by our gate. With over an hour before we would board, we took seats nearby to wait for our flight. Kevin excused himself and I settled and pulled out my Kindle. I preferred actual books, but one could not beat the convenience of an e-reader. I perused my library and decided on *Doctor Sleep* by Stephen King, one of my favorite authors. Completely engrossed in the story, I had not realized so much time had passed. The preliminary announcements for boarding were starting and Kevin had not reappeared. I lowered the e-reader onto my lap and slowly glanced around the nearby vicinity. I spotted him seated in a different section of the gate area, and his back was to me. I shrugged, put away my e-reader, and grabbed my boarding pass. I was in seat 14K, a window seat. *Oh, that's right!* I thought suddenly and inhaled quickly. I remembered Kevin's seat was 14H and according to the online seating chart, someone was sitting between us in 14J. The plan had been to ask the person in 14J to switch. *Not today!* I thought to myself and laughed out loud.

I slid into 14K, placed my personal item under the seat, and plugged my earbuds into the monitor in front of me. I buckled up and settled in for the ten-hour flight back to Chicago. 14J arrived at our row next, and then I noticed Kevin moving down the aisle. I put my earbuds into my ears and reviewed the selection of in-flight entertainment. Still able to see him in my field of view as I looked straight ahead at the monitor, 14*J* looked at both of us as if without words he were asking if we wanted to sit together. Ignoring the silent inquiry, I continued browsing. As far as I was concerned, the seating arrangements for 14*H*, 14*J*, and 14*K* was settled. The boarding announcements commenced and I was giddy with anticipation of my arrival back to Chicago.

By the time we entered customs in Chicago, more than one person was separating myself and Kevin. Having an aisle seat relatively close to the front, Kevin had sprung to his feet and was at the front of the line as soon as the ding sounded and gave permission to remove our seatbelts. Standing in the border control line, I reminded myself again that I needed Global Entry, and reviewed my to do list for the evening. *Still at the airport and already back to business. Goddammit* was my next thought. In my excitement to be back, I forgot Kevin was not leaving Chicago until the next day. The original plan was for him to spend the night at my place and Uber to the airport while I dressed for work. I hoped he was smart enough to know that he was not staying at my place.

After retrieving my bag from the carousel, I exited the airport to find Kevin standing outside. He walked over to me as I entered the chill Chicago air.

"Well," he said, "I guess this is it."

"That it is." I replied.

"I got a hotel room for the night right over here by—"

"Thank the universe you have *some* sense!" I interrupted his statement and lifted a hand of praise towards the air.

Kevin gave me a look of disbelief and stood watching as I walked over to the taxi stand. The attendant at the booth flagged a driver, and a taxi pulled up to where I stood waiting at the curb. The driver placed my bags in the car and Kevin said goodbye as I hopped in the taxi. I gave him a quick wave and closed the door. A toothy grin parted my lips. I did not remember the last time I was so happy to be back in Chicago.

ONE AND DONE

*A*fter dropping my suitcases off at home, I picked up Scrappy from boarding. The attendant walked my tiny dog to me, and Scrappy bounced up and down with excitement. I embraced my pup and welcomed his wet kisses. Back home, my pets reunited, I unpacked my luggage as Sox and Scrappy scurried around the West Loop condo. As I put things away and washed my clothes, I contrasted the excited anticipation I had prior to traveling, with my current relieved return to solitude. I had gained little clarity from Kevin, and although I was thrilled to be back in my own space, the confusion about the relationship's end weighed heavily on my mind. It hurt to think the entire relationship disintegrated when I was just being me. Asserting myself and moving out of my apparent predestined path of passivity made me sassy thereby bruising his fragile ego beyond repair. For a moment, I was sad. RP reminded me of that smirk, and I shuddered.

"Oh well", I said aloud as I sat down at my computer and got to work. I was pleasantly surprised to find most of the agendas and meeting notes for the week were already complete.

"I guess I prepped more than I remembered." I said as I

reviewed the outlines and highlighted the salient features of my plan.

I rolled my chair away from the desk as the colors of sunset painted my office and rarely used guest room. Orange reflected onto my face by the glass encasings of academic achievements that decorated the walls. I spun around in the chair pleased with the work I had done. The sense of accomplishment always put me in a good mood. Even better, it was early, and there was still time to relax before I went to bed.

I went to the kitchen, opened a bottle of red wine, and poured a glass. Walking into the living area with full length windows making up an entire wall of my corner unit, the view of the sunset disappearing behind the Chicago skyline was majestic. I placed my glass of wine atop a coaster on the glass side table before walking across the light hardwood floor to my wall mounted entertainment center set. I turned on my Xbox and took a controller from its charging cradle. I curled up on the heather grey sofa as the startup to *Titanfall* occupied my fifty-five-inch TV screen. I settled into the first-person shooter game and thoughts of Kevin could not have been further away.

Time passed quickly, and I was busy. With my initiatives for the department of Obstetrics and Gynecology at Park Lawn Hospital on Chicago's Southside fully underway, I was like a cat climbing to new heights and felt at home in my role as medical director. A few months later, all the planning and hard work paid off and our department was fully integrated with an electronic documentation system and computerized order entry. I was sharing the news with Fawzia, a friend and coworker, at the end of a busy day in the office when my phone rang. It was a blackout screen. I shook my head.

"I wonder who it is today." I said feigning enthusiasm as I

looked at the name on the black screen, the color signified one thing I knew for sure about men; they always came back. I let out a quick incredulous chuckle, it was Kevin. I showed Fawzia the phone screen.

"Are you gonna answer?" Fawzia asked.

"I'll bite." I replied and answered the call.

"Hello?"

"Hey, Uh, do you know who this is?" Kevin said shakily.

I was surprised to find his voice, once seemingly like silk, was now nails on a chalkboard, and I was instantly irritated.

"My caller ID tends to do the work for me, what's up?"

"Well, I was hoping we could talk." He replied cutting to the chase, perhaps sensing the no nonsense of my tone.

"I'm listening." My curiosity overpowered my irritation.

"I was hoping we could talk. I wanted to explain my behavior in Italy and have an opportunity to apologize."

I rolled my eyes. He was saying what he hoped he could say and not actually saying anything. Irritation was now winning the battle with curiosity.

"I repeat. I'm listening." I said, attempting to control RP's hissing in my voice.

"I was hoping we could talk in person." Kevin said in a tone too full of hope.

"Um."

The um, long and drawn out, did little to convey the disbelief that painted itself over my expression of workplace professionalism.

"How and why did you think that?" I asked.

"I thought I would fly up and we could…" As he spoke my brow furrowed deeper with every word and only one thought kept repeating in my mind. *Why? Why the fuck? Like really, why?* Although the questions were silent, in my mind they were loud and angry roars.

"Rosalyn, are you there?" Kevin's voice asking me a question interrupted the roaring whys.

"Yep. I'm here." I said nodding my head slowly as if he could see the physical affirmation.

"What do you think?" He asked.

I gave his question a deep consideration before answering.

"I think that we can talk over the phone. I also think that there is nothing you could possibly say to me that requires an in-person visit." I explained, annoyed that he wanted to plan a trip to talk while we were on the phone talking.

"I think it's better if we talk in person." He persisted.

"Well, ok, you are entitled to your opinion." Irritation had come out on top. "You called me hoping we could talk, so if there is something you need to say to me, now is the time."

"Well if you don't want to talk in person, I guess I know all I need to know." He spoke. I could hear that he was appalled by my declination of his offer.

"Ok great. Is there anything else?" I asked sarcastically.

"Bye Rosalyn." Kevin said, and I could hear him smirking through the phone.

I hung up and filled Fawzia in on the epilogue to my Italian drama.

"Aren't you curious even a little?" Fawzia asked after I recounted the conversation with my ex.

"A little, which is why I answered the phone in the first place." I responded. "The only thing he could want is to try again, but to come back with stipulations attached to his apology after the way he acted just further lets me know he is not the one for me. My peace means more than answers." I stated emphatically.

"He was going to come up here! That's a lot." She insisted, remembering how smitten I was with Kevin.

"Being great at grand gestures and practiced penance after fucking up and expecting me to drop everything, forgive and forget, does not make you an awesome partner, it makes you manipulative." I said with a shrug.

"Do you think you can forgive him?"

"Sure. I can forgive him, but that does not mean he gets to be a part of my life."

"That's true." Fawzia said, nodding thoughtfully.

"You only get one shot with me, one shot to choose *me*. After that, I will never give you an opportunity to make that choice again; one and done." I said resolutely.

"Oh well Kevin." Fawzia said, speaking loudly as if to Kevin states away. "I don't know what to tell you homie, my girl gave you a chance." We laughed and left the office for the day.

Taking Ashland north towards my neighborhood, break lights stretched as far as the eye could see.

"Good ole Chicago traffic", I sighed.

With red lights decorating the interior of my Camry, I thought about Kevin's call and could not believe the audacity of this man child. A passive participant during our entire trip indulging in infantile indifference instead of adult communication, *now, four* months later, Kevin wanted to take reconciliatory action. What really made RP arch her back and erect her tail was that he fully expected to ingratiate himself into my life and for me to welcome him with open arms.

"Who does that?" I said aloud, my mood now matching the color of the lights. I knew the answer to my question was almost everyone. I had seen it play out time and time again. From friends to my sisters, I had listened as the women in my life had described what amounted to domestic warfare. Despite repeated injuries from the minefields of infidelity and emotional manipulation, they removed the shrapnel from their hearts and continued attempts to mend their relationships. I wanted desperately for them to love themselves more, to free themselves from their relationship hamster wheel of hurt and reconciliation. I was often told "That is love Rosalyn. You forgive and keep working on things."

"If that is what love looks like, I do not want it." I said aloud and tightened my grip on the steering wheel. I was seeing red as my thoughts drifted away from the traffic.

THE MUSIC BLARED FROM THE SIX FOOT HIGH SPEAKERS. THE BLUE Dolphin was packed and Nomi and I danced wildly in the crowd. Six months into residency, it was my first weekend off in a while and I purged my stress leaving it all on the dance floor.

"I'm going to get another drink." I yelled to Nomi over the music.

She shot me a thumbs up in response.

I walked over to the bar and raised a hand to get the bartender's attention. After ordering, I stood at the bar bopping my head to the beat when I saw him. Tall, fair skinned, with blue eyes, and a huge fro, he approached the bar and stood next to me.

"Hi." I said with a smile and eyes filled with curiosity.

"Hey." He greeted me and returned the smile. His perfectly aligned teeth complemented his oddly handsome face.

After brief banter at the bar, Carter followed me to the dance floor and that was the beginning of our love affair. Carter and I did everything together. We both believed in the motto "work hard, play harder" and we definitely played well together. We would party into the wee hours of the morning and our chemistry was unmatched.

In addition to his looks, Carter had an attractive mind. He was well educated and well versed on a myriad of topics and our conversations would last and last twisting and turning until neither of us knew what exactly we were talking about. We shared everything. He knew all of my stories. He knew all of my hopes, dreams, and triggers.

Carter and I were discussing so called "struggle love" as we rode through the Chicago city streets. I ranted about dealbreakers and the importance of knowing when and how to walk away. Carter nodded in agreement. It had been three years since that night at the Blue Dolphin and with residency at an end, and my initial weeks as an attending going smoothly, we decided that the transition would be a good time for us to move in together. I had lived alone since college and my home had become a safe space free from life's stressors. Although I loved Carter, I was nervous about sharing space, but decided to take this next step with him.

As we arrived at a contender in our search for a new home, a growing sense of unease settled in my stomach. Walking through the beautiful South Loop apartment, the unease grew into an intense pain and I winced with every step. I excused myself to the bathroom before finishing the tour and after regurgitating my lunch, I figured it was just something I ate.

The next morning, after saying goodbye to Carter and wishing him a productive day at work, the sense of queasiness returned. I shook it off and prepared for my day at the office. Sitting at the desk of my Southside office space, my stomach still in knots, an overwhelming feeling of Déjà vu washed over me. When my phone rang, I knew it would be Carter.

"Hey babe!" I said cheerfully. "You just caught me; I was about to go see a patient."

"Hey!" He said. "I'm glad I know your number by heart. I left my phone at your place." As he spoke, I knew his words before he said them, and I could picture his phone in my room on the windowsill.

"I think it is on the windowsill in your bedroom." He continued.

"Yeah, I know." I said lost in thought. A clear picture of the phone and its location was visible in my mind, but I did not know how I was so sure. I must have unconsciously noticed it that morning.

"Ok, well I'm coming by after work to pick it up before I meet up with my mom."

"Yeah ok, sounds good." I said and hung up the phone. Dismissing the sense of familiarity, I got to work.

Arriving home, I had forgotten about my stomach and the mornings eerie Déjà vu, when I entered my bedroom and it all came rushing back. I walked to the phone and looked at it on the windowsill. I knew I was going to pick it up before I did, and the moment reminded me of a distant dream. Carter's phone was locked, and having never asked for the code, I watched as my fingers moved across the keypad entering the passcode in a single attempt. How did I know that? I wondered as the gurgling in my stomach intensified. I scrolled to his messages. What I saw turned the gurgle into a surge and I rushed to the bathroom.

As the emotional turmoil made its way through my digestive tract, I scrolled through message after message learning of past and current encounters Carter had with other women. The texts ranged from subtle subtext, alluding to physical intimacies they shared, to overt sexting.

I was devastated. The course of our relationship seemed to flash before my eyes and tears blurred my vision. The deep sense of betrayal gave way to anger which pacified my agitated bowels. Frenzied and furious, I tore through my home and threw anything belonging to Carter into a trash bag. He would arrive any minute to get his phone, and I would be outside waiting.

He was approaching the gated Southside apartment complex just as I was walking through the courtyard. I opened the gate and stopped him on the sidewalk leading up to my building. He started talking before I could.

"Damn, I have had a bad day. I got a boot on my car. I'm late to meet my mom, and—"

"Welp, your day is about to get worse." I interrupted. Carter looked at me with curiosity in his eyes, finally noticing the trash bag in my hands.

"I found your phone." I continued. "I went through it. There is a lot of interesting reading material in there. Your text messages were particularly enlightening." I said scowling and making no attempts to hide the rage I found myself in.

"I don't know what you are talking about." He said, his skin tone betraying his words as a flush came to his face undermining his lie.

"Boy, I am a doctor, I think I can read." I shot back angrily. "Here are your things." I dropped the bag at his feet and turned to the gate.

"Rosalyn, wait." Carter pleaded.

"Wait, for what, Carter?" I asked, not looking for a response as I unlocked the gate, entered the courtyard, and walked back to my apartment.

For months after our confrontation on the sidewalk, Carter tried repeatedly to garner my favor. He sent gifts and made calls acknowledging his wrongdoings and promising change. Every time I spoke to him, I could feel my heart strings pulling and tugging, a part of me wanting desperately to give him another chance. Carter was aware of my triggers and had known the pain of my youth yet chose to betray my trust. My response to his attempts at persuasion was always the same. "I accept your apology, but I can no longer be with you. I am not going to willingly sign up for a life of looking through your phone, or over my shoulder."

A CAR HORN ALERTING ME THAT TRAFFIC WAS NOW MOVING brought me back to the here and now. I waved my hand in recognition and pressed the gas. Entering my West Loop condo, I thought of Kevin, and how I may never know what really happened in Italy. It did not matter; an explanation would not change anything. I greeted Sox and Scrappy, and as I changed out of office attire a quote came to mind: "When people show you who they are, believe them." Those were words that I had lived by long before I heard Maya Angelou say them. On our ill-fated Italian journey, Kevin had shown me who he was, and I was at peace moving on with my life without him.

ROCKSTAR

Where is it? I thought as I rummaged through my office closet. The organized chaos that made up the spacious walk-in was in more disarray than I remembered. Standing on my tip toes and reaching into the corner of the top shelf, I finally grazed the object of my hunt. "There you are." I said as I used my fingertips to slide it into my grasp. Scrappy yelped as I retrieved the item and lowered my heel onto his tail.

"Sorry Scraps!" I shrieked.

"You are always all up on me!" I exclaimed as the little dog looked up at me in confusion. Sox popped him on his head for good measure.

My bucket list box was where I kept pictures and reminders of grand adventures. Once I had the experience, I would replace the aspirational image with something to represent its completion. I sat on the dark grey convertible sofa and placed the box on my lap. With my thirty fifth birthday coming up I knew the contents would provide inspiration. With only five days separating my birthday from the sibling's, as children our birthdays were celebrated together. One year we became "too old for all that" and then there were no celebrations at all. After moving to Chicago, my birthday became a holiday, and for the last five years, I had embarked on an international adventure. Kevin and I planned to spend my birthday together this year, but those plans proved premature, and now I needed new ones.

I opened the lid and inspected the items inside. South Africa, the Galapagos, Australia, and Egypt, were all places I had yet to visit. They were amazing options, but it was mid-April, my birthday was six weeks away, and I only had one week off. Pushing aside photos, my scuba diving certification, and skydiving discs, I continued perusing the box's contents. I was turning the pages of my old passport when I noticed a colorful folded flyer. As I unfolded and studied the flyer, my eyes widened, and a devilish grin spread across my face. My ringing phone interrupted my quickly turning wheels.

"Well, looky here! Looky here!" I said greeting my caller.

My hello was met with genuine laughter. I laughed too.

"What's up Rockstar!" Marvin said.

"Hey friend!" I said excitedly, drawing out the hey. "Long time."

Marvin and I had known each other for years. He was one of the "Grays" in my life. Usually born from lust, my relationships with the Grays surpassed sex and became fulfilling friendships characterized by open and unfiltered communication. In my relationships with the Grays, I did not bother myself with expectations that these men were to fit into my life in a particular way. I did not need a promise of forever to enjoy and live in the moments we shared together.

My relationship with Marvin was one of cat and mouse, each of us taking turns as hunter and prey. Initially, it was I who ensnared him. I came across his profile while scrolling through Instagram. A series of random clicks led me to his smiling and insanely handsome face.

"I am going to meet this man." I told Megan as we sat on the balcony of my West Loop apartment years before. I had just moved in, and after breaking up with Carter I was looking for a distraction. Marvin was my type of distraction. We had liked a lot of each other's pictures over the past few weeks, but that was as far as our flirtation had gone. I showed her the pictures in his Instagram profile.

"Yeah girl, he is *fine*." She said with emphasis on the word fine. "Why don't you slide into his DM's?" She asked.

"Nah, not my style. The universe will create an opportunity for us to meet." I responded.

Megan looked at me with skepticism.

"It'll happen." I said nodding assuredly.

Weeks later I attended the Chosen Few House Music Picnic on Chicago's Southside. After getting out of the cab, I crossed the street to join the crowd waiting for admittance into Jackson Park. As I approached the group of people, I saw him, and he was just as handsome as he was in photos. I smiled.

"Marvin!" I walked up to him casually, saying his name in a tone that suggested we had known each other for years.

He searched my face and responded with friendly confusion.

"Hey." He greeted me and then politely added, "I'm sorry. I am blanking on your name."

"You know me as Star." I said and then extended my hand. "My real name is Rosalyn."

"Yea! Star! Nice to meet you in person. I'm Marvin."

Now, four years later, we were commonplace in each other's lives, more intimate than friends, but neither of us seeking clarity or commitment. Defining the relationship was neither desired nor was it a requirement for our constantly deepening connection.

We were catching up on life events and I filled him in on my breakup.

"Man, I'm sorry to hear that. I know you liked dude." He said.

"I did, but it's all good." I replied.

"You know what's crazy though, I can't really picture you in a serious relationship." He stated.

"Gee, thanks Marvin!" I said sarcastically with laughter in my voice.

"Nah, please don't take offense. I am just saying, I call you a Rockstar because that is how I see you. It is like you cannot be bothered with settling down."

"I cannot see myself *settling* for anything!" I exclaimed. "Besides, settling and having a life partner are not mutually inclusive." I stated.

"They don't have to be." He said flirtatiously.

I guess I am the mouse today. I thought and blushed. Marvin had that effect on me.

"Exactly." I said and continued, "Let me tell you what I just decided to do for my birthday!"

It was his turn to blush.

After hanging up with Marvin, I went to my desk and turned on my computer to research my chosen birthday destination. I pulled up the website. Its logo, two mermaids facing each other with a pitchfork between them piqued my interest as I scrolled through photos and read descriptions and testimonials. My birthday weekend fell on the Memorial Day holiday this year and the robust activity calendar indicated the resort expected a high turnout. Memorial Day Mocha Madness, an event spanning the entire week of my vacation, caught my attention and I clicked for more details. I giggled as I reviewed the itinerary. Sox hopped into my lap and purred.

"I could not agree more!" I said aloud and picked up my cell phone. I knew the perfect person to invite along.

AFTER LANDING IN MONTEGO BAY, JAMAICA, WE HOPPED IN A CAB and settled in for the hour drive to our destination. Along the way, we had lively conversation about what to expect when we got there. Other than what I had read, I had no idea what was in store. She told me only I would have her engaged in an experience like this one. I laughed and thanked her for joining me on the excursion.

Megan and I hopped out of the cab and entered the lobby of the Indulgence II, an all-inclusive clothing optional resort. Check-in was seamless and an attendant gathered our luggage. He walked us to our suite, pointing out all the amenities the resort had to offer along the way. The resort was quiet. Raindrops decorated the leaves of plants lining the wet concrete walkways. Drops falling from palm trees tapped us as we walked along the damp path.

"We must have just missed the rain." I said aloud.

"That's probably why no one is outside right now." Megan speculated.

The attendant stopped at a door on the ground floor near the pool and took the key out of a small envelope.

"We are in a great location." I said.

"Yes." The attendant agreed. "You are not far from the dining area and only steps away from the nude pool complete with a swim up bar and a hot tub."

We entered the immaculate minimally decorated room. The furniture was contemporary and sleek. A large window made up the back wall of the room and we had a gorgeous view of the ocean. A back door led to a private terrace. The double queen beds made up with white linen, were inviting after a morning of travel. After tipping the attendant, I flopped onto one of the beds and lay on my back. I laughed when I noticed the mirrors on the ceiling.

"It's my birthday!" I squealed as soon as I opened my eyes the next morning. Megan laughed.

"Happy birthday Rosalyn!"

"We are going to jump in with both feet today!" I said enthusiastically. The rain returned the day before and instead of mingling, we opted for in room dining and relaxation.

"Let's do it!" Megan responded.

"First, breakfast."

Leaving our room and heading to the dining area, the one place on the resort where clothing was mandatory, I noticed it was a beautiful day. It was sunny and hot which was my favorite forecast. The resort was much busier than it had been upon our arrival. People walked and talked amongst themselves, greeting passersby. There was a buzz in the air, and everyone appeared cheerful and upbeat. This is going to be a fun day. I thought to myself. Breakfast was expansive and offered everything imaginable. The food was delicious and after having our fill we headed back to our room to disrobe.

The plan was to spend the day frolicking at the nude pool party. Standing in the mirror wearing nothing but my birthday suit, I looked at my body and studied my perceived imperfections. Clasping gold body jewelry around my neck, the coolness of the metal erected my nipples and I continued to survey my body. I especially noticed the scars, keloids that told tales of my skin's history. The origins of my skin struggles came to mind as I traced the keloid near my elbow on my left arm. I remembered the events exactly two decades before that put it there. I remembered how I felt with the realization that my skin had changed forever. The scar underneath my right breast was barely noticeable as it peaked through the sparkling body accessory. I turned around and looked over my shoulder at the faded line across my right shoulder blade and the back of my right arm.

I had become comfortable with my scars. Oftentimes, I forgot they were there, and was only reminded of them when questioned by those gaining purview of my naked body. The more visible scars would occasionally gain the attention of strangers in public, but I learned to become impervious to the piercing eyes of others. With memories of the source of my "keloid skin", I was eternally grateful that the unsightly blemishes were not on my face. Focusing on the positive, I smiled at my reflection in the mirror, shook off the memories, and Megan and I walked outside.

The nude pool was large with a swim up bar located on one end. There were barstools around its perimeter, and we decided the bar was a good place to start. Megan and I pranced proudly through the swimming pool deck. People of all shapes, sizes, and ages were leisurely lounging in the nude. Some relaxed in chairs by the pool while others occupied the inviting water, soaking up the sun on floaties and sitting at in-pool dining areas. The water was cool and felt good on my bare skin. We waded through the pool and took seats on stools at the bar.

"Hello!" The bartender greeted us cheerfully.

"Hello!" We said back in unison.

"What will you ladies have today?" The bartender asked, his Jamaican accent made his words sound melodic.

"Let's do shots!" Megan said.

"Let's!" I agreed and asked the bartender, "What type of shot would you like to make us?"

"It's her birthday!" Megan chimed in.

"Blowjob shots for you ladies then." He said with a sly smile and started mixing ingredients.

Passing us two shot glasses each filled with a "Blowjob" the bartender said, "These shots are done without using your hands." We laughed, and he gave us a little wink.

Placing my hands behind my back, I wrapped my lips around the shot glass, created a suction, and tipped my head back. I repeated my actions for the second.

"Woo!" I exclaimed and gave Megan a high five. "Happy birthday!" She screamed.

"It's your birthday?" An unfamiliar voice asked.

Turning to see a handsome group of people, I responded. "Yes. It is my birthday!"

"I think we need more shots!" He said and the small group that had formed around Megan and I erupted into a chorus of "Yes!".

The bartender lined up more shots. Music started blaring from the speakers as we downed our drinks and everyone in the pool area started to cheer.

The nude pool party was underway. The bar area cleared as people rushed into the pool. Creating a dance space for myself in the center of the pool facing the DJ booth, I moved to the beat and my body's motions became in sync with the rhythm. I welcomed dance partners both male and female into my space and was euphoric as our bodies collided. I looked around at the picture of jubilation and was thrilled to be a part of the scintillating atmosphere. Best birthday ever! I thought as the Blowjob buzz tickled my senses and I danced naked in a sea of people.

My week at Indulgence II was a blur of excellent food and entertainment, nude parties, leather, lingerie, strippers, new acquaintances, and sexy themed nights. By the time Megan and I were boarding our flight back to Chicago, I was relaxed and satiated. I had been to the closest thing to a utopia with its cornucopia of pleasures and had indulged in them all. I felt more confident in my body than ever and had developed a heightened sense of comfort in my scarred skin.

I closed my eyes as we ascended to cruising altitude and I let my thoughts drift. My energy was high as I relived moments from my thirty fifth birthday experience. I felt like a Rockstar. My thoughts turned to Marvin. "You can't be bothered with settling down." He had said to me. He was right. I refused to believe that I had to settle for anything. Having just accomplished another bucket box adventure, I smiled with a sense of pride. My heart had always been wild, and I promised myself long ago I would not let anyone crush that spirit.

13

DAREDEVIL

"Rosalyn, get down!" Mari yelled.

I held the thick tree trunk in a bear hug, one foot preparing for its step to the next branch as my friend shouted from below. I looked down at her as I readied myself to continue the climb.

"I'm not even that high yet!" I said as Mari stood in the grass surrounding the tree looking at me with worry on her young face.

I had always thought the tree in the front yard of my new neighborhood home looked perfect for climbing. I had watched numerous times as Kitt and Frizz quickly climbed to the top, and eventually made their way back down. Although I had been told time and again that little girls should not climb trees, this tree called out to me, its sturdy trunk and wide branches coaxing me to come out and play. With catlike agility, I climbed higher until my friend's anxious cries were just a whisper. I straddled a thick branch, caught my breath, and sat for a while enjoying the bird's eye view. Soon, the anxiety of being found out disrupted the serenity of the moment. *I had better get down before Momma gets home.* I thought to myself and prepared for my descent. Halfway down, my foot slipped on the tree's trunk and I lost my grip on the branch above my head. I landed on the ground with a thud. My back's impact on the grass knocked the wind out of me and everything went dark.

Muffled crying and sparks of light broke through the darkness. Slowly my senses returned and I gasped for air. Through the lessening fog, I could see my friends face distorted with tears. Her ten-year-old body trembled with worry. I lay on my back staring silently at the tree from which I had just fallen. Then I started laughing. I laughed and could not stop. My hysterical cackles were contagious and soon Mari and I were both lying in the grass consumed with laughter.

My childhood dance with daring deeds earned me the nickname Evel Knievel. As the years passed, my adventure jones intensified. During my adolescence, rollercoasters were my favorite and I frequented the local theme park. I would walk hurriedly to the winding queue and watch wide eyed as the rollercoaster zipped overhead. My excited anticipation was almost uncontrollable as I awaited my turn. I would hop in the seat, pull the harness down tightly onto my chest, and bounce my legs, eagerly awaiting the start of the ride. The clicking of the rollercoaster inching forward was enough for me to squeal with enthusiasm and as the coaster made its ascent a wide grin would appear on my face. At the apex of the climb, I would release my hands from the harness and lift them in the air readying myself for the drop. As the coaster made its speeding descent, I would hope for airtime and would laugh and scream simultaneously when I was lifted out of my seat. When the ride stopped and harnesses were lifted, I would scramble back to the line and do it all over again.

A SEEKER OF EXCITEMENT, I TOOK ANY OPPORTUNITY PRESENTED TO me to push my limits. As a part of orientation prior to the start of medical school, I participated in MOO, Medical school Outdoor

Orientation. MOO trips provided an opportunity to bond with classmates and relax before embarking on our medical school journey. Among the options presented to us, only one stood out to me, and it was whitewater rafting. I had not gone whitewater rafting before, and up until that point my adrenaline fixes were limited to rollercoasters and ejection seats.

Following a three-hour bus ride, we arrived at the Ocoee rafting center. After signing waivers, we took seats at long benches for the introduction to whitewater rafting and safety class. The room was filled with racks of oars with red, blue, and yellow paddles as well as crates of safety equipment. We watched a brief video and at its end, the instructors explained terms our trip leaders would use along the way. Paddle left. Paddle right. Dig. Brace. Lean in. We learned about flips and what to do if you "took a swim". After our class, we gathered equipment and our protective gear. I snapped my red life jacket together, put on a red safety helmet, and got a paddle. As I milled about the preparation area waiting for everyone to ready themselves, I overheard bits of conversation between guides.

"The rapids are little fast today. Not smoker levels by any means but definitely running fast."

And another. "Yeah, I plan to take it easy on my group today." The second guide said looking towards the group I planned to raft with. I crinkled my nose. I wanted the full experience and taking it easy did not sound like fun.

"We need a fifth." It was Peter's voice. He and three other male classmates were looking for an addition to their raft.

Perfect! I thought. My raft had enough people with or without me, and I became the fifth member to Peter's team. Peter, Josh, Reggie, Gary, and I followed our tour guide as he led us to the "put in". We entered our paddle boat, sat down, and slipped our feet underneath the air tubes in front of us as instructed, making sure not to jam them in too deeply just in case we took a "swim".

We were taking the Upper Ocoee River trip, home of the 1996

Olympic Whitewater. As the speed picked up along the river, my pulse quickened. My breathing became more rapid. I welcomed the sensations and the burst of adrenaline felt good.

"Dig. Dig!" The trip guide yelled. We responded by pushing our paddles deep into the water and forcefully pulling them through. As we sped along bends, the wild waters collided with our bucking raft. We whooped and hollered as the raft maneuvered the waves. "Paddle left. *LEFT!*" The guide's voice commanded. As we were placing our paddles into the water, the guide's instructions changed to *"LEAN IN! LEAN IN! BRACE!"*

I quickly placed my paddle in the boat and braced myself by curling my body and head inward toward the center of the raft. The raft hit a rock obscured by the rapids. The impact jolted the raft, and I was airborne. I hit the water violently, and the rushing rapids took me under. My helmeted head struck a rock and my body twisted and turned beneath the river's surface. Careening through the rushing river, I smashed my sternum into another large rock before a standing wave propelled me back to the water's surface. I took in quick shallow breaths and kept my feet up. The red and yellow safety boat bobbed in and out of view as I fought against the current. Despite my life jacket, I was taken back under and found myself trapped beneath the capsized raft. Facing the upside-down raft, I found an air pocket and gasped for air. I pushed myself away from the raft and resurfaced as the safety boat made its way closer. I grabbed the outstretched paddle, climbed into the rescue raft, and was reunited with my team.

"Rosalyn, are you alright?" My rafting crew asked. They looked at me with anxious eyes and their foreheads were creased with worry.

"That was fucking awesome!" I replied with a broad smile and a wild look in my eyes. We all laughed.

Whitewater rafting had been invigorating. I had been thrown into the rapids, and like a cat falling from a tree, I righted myself and landed on my feet. The terror of the events of the day proved exhilarating and I felt like I had nine lives. I enjoyed the rush that accompanied accomplishing adrenaline filled pursuits and over the years I continued elevating the risk. The wristbands, flyers, and photos I kept and added to my bucket box served as a reminder to live life unscripted.

Introspection led me to a deeper purpose for my actions, and thrill seeking became my way to overcome fears. The first flight I took as a teen was wrought with turbulence. I squeezed the armrests tightly with sweaty palms as the plane jostled my body in the seat. The ding followed by an announcement to return to seats and strap on our safety belts momentarily quieted the chatter of my high school senior classmates, and those standing returned to their seats. My stomach's churning was as violent as the jerky flight, and I watched nervously as flight staff attempted to reassure passengers. The plane lurched sideways, and the force was enough to knock me into Joy who was sitting beside me praying quietly. A few of my classmates yelped. Moments later, oxygen masks popped out from compartments above our heads.

"We're all going to die!" A girl stood up and yelled.

The group of friends she was with burst into laughter.

I grabbed the bobbing yellow mask and placed it on my face and closed my eyes tight. My heart raced and I was breathing too fast. Joy and I grabbed each other's hands.

The Germantown High School senior class of 1999 arrived in Cancun Mexico safely that day, but the flight experience had its lingering effects. Each time I flew after that, the whirring of a plane's engine and the mechanical hum of wings preparing to take flight would reignite the turbulence in my gut. A sense of anxiety would wash over me and until the aircraft landed at its destination, I was afraid. Fear was a foreign and unsettling feeling and I hated that I could not control the emotion. My father had told me never be afraid of anything. I was determined to mind his words and to become fearless.

. . .

I drove slowly, the crunching of the unpaved road provided the only soundtrack as I looked for my destination. The building seemed to appear out of nowhere, and I turned into Chicagoland Skydiving Center. It was a beautiful day in Chicago, warmer than usual for early May and I was thankful for good weather. I had mentally prepared myself for this challenge, and I was happy a weather delay would not interrupt my goal for the day.

After signing in and signing waivers, I listened closely to the instructors as they reviewed safety instructions. I was then strapped into a harness and led out onto the airstrip. The closer I got to the prop plane; I could feel the gurgling start to rise from within. Not today. I thought as I got into the plane. The plane was small and had two benches, one on either side of the cabin. The instructors sat down first, and the tandem divers sat in their laps. Crammed into the limited space, tethered to my instructor, and sitting knee to knee with other participants, I felt my anxiety rise as we started our ascent. The whirring of the propeller made my head spin and my palms dripped with sweat.

Once the plane reached the 14,000 feet jump altitude, we crouched inside as one by one participants and instructors in tandem disappeared from the aircraft. It was my turn; I lowered my goggles onto my face and tightened the straps. We inched closer to the edge of the doorway and looking out from the aircraft, I could see nothing but blue sky and green blocks of grass below. My skydive instructor yelled over the wind to give last minute instructions.

"On three!" He shouted and started the count. "One, two—"

Three never came. Before I knew it, we were out of the plane. The instructor tapped my shoulder and I put my body into position, both arms out and up like wings and my knees bent at a ninety-degree angle. The wind rushed into my face at over one hundred miles per hour. The force of the air entering my lungs was suffocating. I quickened the pace of my breaths to accommodate the wind's onslaught. I had prepared to feel a drop in my stomach, but there was none. There was also no gurgling or churning sense of anxiety. I was having fun. The sixty second free fall felt much longer. When my tandem instructor deployed the parachute and I could hear something other than the wind, the first sound I heard was my own excited laughter. I took off the goggles and enjoyed the panoramic views as we made our floating descent. It was peaceful and beautiful and in perfect contrast to the jaw dropping free fall. When I made it to the ground, I knew I was going skydiving again. I also knew that my anxiety surrounding flying was gone forever.

Now, as I said goodbye to Jamaica, still buzzing from baring all, I marveled over the adventures I have had. I had conquered my fears of flying, the ocean, and enclosed spaces with skydiving, scuba diving, and caving, and each activity fortified my adventuresome spirit. I cozied up in the airplane seat with a neck pillow and blanket and mentally reviewed the contents of my bucket box. The remaining postcards and paper scraps were now outnumbered by memorabilia. As the plane soared smoothly through the air, the sounds of the engine now like a lullaby, I closed my eyes and dreamed of my next exciting venture.

14

RECREATIONAL USE ONLY

*D*ing. The sound followed by the bustling of people gathering their belongings woke me from my in-flight nap. I followed suit and made my way through the airport. After saying goodbye to Megan, I journeyed home by cab feeling rejuvenated and refreshed. Scrappy excitedly greeted me at the door, when I entered my twenty first floor condo. I bent down to pick up my pup and he planted wet kisses on my face.

"Aww Scraps, I missed you too!" Sox looked up from her food bowl and meowed before returning to her meal.

"Hello to you too Sox!" I said with a smile. I entered the kitchen to find a note from my pet sitter letting me know what a "good boy and girl" my "fur babies" were while I was away.

"Thanks for behaving yourselves!" I said aloud to my animals. Scrappy bounced excitedly at my feet while Sox sauntered away.

I went to my bedroom, unpacked, and prepared clothing for the work week. I removed my bucket list box from its new home on the shelf of my bedroom closet. I was placing the event wristbands and the folded schedule of sensual activities from my birthday celebration inside, when my phone rang. I smiled as the name shown on the caller ID.

"Hey you!" I answered with enthusiasm.

"What's up Rockstar?" Marvin responded.

"A repeat call so soon? To what do I owe the pleasure?" I teased. Marvin and I would go on streaks, conversing and seeing each other consistently for several months at a time before one break in communication led to an interaction drought.

He laughed. "How was your trip?"

"OMG!" I said dramatically, drawing out the letters. "It was amazing!" I emphasized the word amazing by increasing the octave of my voice.

"Tell me about it." He said, matching my energy.

I filled him in on the delectable details of my week of debauchery at Indulgence II.

"Wow. That sounds like quite a trip." He said with laughter in his voice.

"It was literally the best birthday trip ever!" I exclaimed.

"How did you come up with this idea?" He asked.

"You know I am an adrenaline junky. I like pushing myself outside of comfort zones. This experience was an item on my list."

"Is there anything left on this list of yours?" Marvin asked.

"It's actually a box, and I'm looking through it now. I have a few trips I want to take, then there's night scuba diving and shark diving."

"Shark diving! Heck naw! Count me out." He laughed.

While Marvin elaborated on his fears of the ocean's unknown, I was lost in thought. A small piece of folded lined paper caught my attention as I rummaged through the bucket list box, looking for still unaccomplished feats. Unfolding the paper and reading the words inside distracted me from my conversation with Marvin.

"Rosalyn, are you still there?" Marvin asked.

"Yes, I am here. Shark diving, right. I would go cage diving first and work my way up to free diving."

"Girl, you are crazy!"

"Nah, not crazy. I refuse to tiptoe through life." I responded distractedly.

"You sound deflated. You were just on ten a second ago. Are you okay?" Marvin always had the ability to detect the fluctuations in my tone and mood.

"I found this slip of paper in my bucket box. I am not sure why I even put it there, it would be better in one of my journals. But anyway, it now has me thinking about stuff other than adventure."

"What is it?" He asked.

"During our first year in medical school, we were asked to write down our deepest fears. Some of my classmates shared theirs aloud. Most were phobias like heights, drowning, fire, or related to having a bad patient outcome. My fear was that I would accomplish and acquire everything I wanted in life yet have no one to share that life with. Reading those words brought back memories of Kevin and blew my mood a bit."

"I told you before, I think you intimidate these dudes." Marvin offered.

"Man, if I had a nickel!" I exclaimed and then asked, "What specifically about me is so intimidating?"

"Shit, Rosalyn, everything!" Marvin said, his tone exaggerating the word everything. He then continued. "You are a doctor, which means you probably are going to make more money. You have had a wealth of worldly experiences; they cannot really introduce you to anything. Really, it is a problem with ego, and the thought that they do not have anything to bring to the table."

"So, what? I am not supposed to experience anything in life, and wait for a romantic partner to do things with? That's silly." I replied.

He chuckled. "Nah, I'm not saying that. I am just saying, all these things make you different, and different is attractive, but at the same time it can be scary."

"Are you trying to tell me you are afraid of me Marvin?" I asked coyly, pawing at him, and feigning modesty.

"Nah, I adore you." He said.

"But," we said simultaneously.

"You don't want kids." He stated.

I already knew the answer. I told Marvin I did not want children soon after we met. Only wanting a physical interaction, I had not cared about his opinion. Now, our relationship had become something different, and I had grown fond of the man Marvin had become. Watching his ambition lead to his exponential growth over the years was inspiring. Although his opinion did not change my perspective, I sometimes fantasized about how things could be if I wanted different.

An audible sigh escaped my lips.

"I don't want kids." I said and shrugged.

"Not even one?" Marvin asked playfully.

I laughed and answered. "Not even one. Why do people say that? Like one child isn't the same full-time life altering responsibility?"

Marvin laughed. "I know right." He said, and then asked gently, "Rosalyn, why don't you want kids?"

"How much time you got?" I joked.

"I'm off today." He responded. I laughed and told him my tale.

I WAS EIGHT YEARS OLD WHEN MY ELDEST SISTER GAVE BIRTH TO HER first child, my parents' first grandchild, and my first nephew. By the time I was fourteen, I had two nieces and two nephews, and now, I had seven. Through my young lenses, I was exposed to the rigors of life with an infant. Taking care of the little bundles of joy was not a rose colored picture. Watching my sisters navigate the never-ending role of service while pursuing careers did little to kindle my maternal instincts. Their husbands offered little co-parenting support and often acted like additional children. After the dissolution of their marriages, the role of caregiver fell to my sisters alone and they were consumed by motherhood. Having children was far from the fairytale portrayed by baby dolls and television specials. For me, it had become synonymous with loss of self.

A built-in babysitter, I was happy to provide even a small amount of relief and my sisters welcomed any help I could offer. During the infancy stages, I did not enjoy the task. I would cringe when the tiny mouths of my nieces and nephews produced loud and piercing cries. When the repetitive cycle of feeding, burping, and changing failed to quiet them, I would be at my wits end, and their screams sapped the energy from my body. As the years went by, interactions with my nieces and nephews became more enjoyable. Their blooming personalities made playtime fun, but I was always elated when my time as caregiver would come to an end.

During my teens, at a time when I was considering sex, unintended pregnancy was on the top of my cons list. My mother repeatedly assured me that she would "put me out" and that I would have to "figure it out" on my own if I were to become pregnant. I believed her. I was sure that if I became pregnant before finishing high school, it would mean the loss of every plan I had made for my life. I was sixteen and in eleventh grade when I spoke to a group of my friends during lunch and told them of my plans to get birth control.

They responded with "I heard birth control makes you gain weight." "I heard they have too many side effects."

"Well, gaining a few pounds is better than gaining a whole baby." I replied. "So, if you want to come with me, meet me at my car after school."

I waited at my car for ten minutes after the last bell for the day. No takers. I thought, as I got in and drove to Planned Parenthood. I was nervous when I entered the tall office building in downtown Memphis.

My sister, Linda, agreed to accompany me, and I was thankful for her presence as I entered the office space. After checking in, my sister and I sat in the lobby. I picked up brochures and read about STD's, breast exams, and contraception. When my name was called, I met with a nurse practitioner and received a detailed consultation about birth control options. She gave thorough answers to my questions and when I elected to start the birth control pill, I was confident with my choice. My experience at Planned Parenthood was empowering. I felt in control of my reproductive health and my future. I felt safer knowing there would be no unwanted pregnancy, and I could finish school without the worry of having to look for a new home. I took those pills every day at the same time as instructed and carried an alarm as a reminder. Since that time, I have explored the full range of contraceptive options and I never leave home without my Mirena IUD.

Following my breakup with Carter, the first thought I had was, *Thank the universe I did not get pregnant!* I realized then I did not feel a connection to the role of motherhood. I doubted if I ever had maternal instincts at all. Now at thirty-five, it seemed that other people's desires for me to reproduce outweighed any concern of my own.

"You still don't have kids?"

"When are you going to get married and have children?"

People gawked at my answer of simple disinterest.

Deciding on life without children made dating challenging and awkward. "What kind of woman doesn't want children?" was a common question from the dating pool. I was aware that for most, partnership and procreation were inextricably linked, and I had come to accept that my life's desires were perceived as selfish. I made no attempts to change the perceptions of anyone I dated, and I knew that although some stated that they could change my mind, I would not be swayed.

"Ultimately, I think you have to want children enough to do it alone." I said to Marvin after giving him a brief but detailed run down of salient moments in my life. "People leave, die, or otherwise abandon you, and children are work. I work enough. I want to live a life without that responsibility."

"Children are a lot of work. Your understanding of that makes you well suited to be a mother." Marvin said thoughtfully.

"My understanding of that lets me know that children and the life I want for myself do not go hand in hand. I'm good with being the cool aunt."

"Damn. I can't even get you pregnant on accident." Marvin responded jokingly.

I laughed. "Nope. Not at all. My reproductive system is for recreational use only." We laughed.

"That's a shame." Marvin said, "We would have some cute kids."

I laughed. "My fur babies are cute enough for me."

After Marvin and I said our goodbyes, I put the scrap of paper back in the bucket list box, closed the lid, and replaced the box on the shelf in my closet. I was proud of my life's journey and I accepted that its winding road has sparked my desires for different. There were many ways to have fulfillment in life and I appreciated my self-awareness surrounding motherhood. Everything was not meant for everyone, and I had learned that not everyone was meant for motherhood.

Scrappy's whimpers interrupted my thoughts. Sox is probably beating him up again. I thought as I exited my bedroom and followed the sounds of my dog's cries. Scrappy paced in a nervous circle outside the guest bathroom door. I knelt and rubbed his head and his whimpers morphed to small barks. Looking toward the slightly cracked bathroom door, I noticed black fur. I pushed the door open slowly.

"Sox, what are you doing in here?" I asked softly and turned on the light.

A small mew answered my question. I looked down to see Sox lying on her side, not moving, her shallow breaths barely perceptible.

"Sox!" I yelped when I noticed the blood dripping from her tongue which protruded slightly from her open mouth.

"Oh no!" I said and tears came rushing to my eyes.

I scooped Sox from the bathroom floor and into her carrier and rushed her to the vet. They quickly whisked Sox away to run tests and my stomach turned with anticipation as I sat crying silently in the waiting room.

"Rosalyn?" The veterinarian appeared and called me to the back.

As she explained my cat's prognosis and the recommended euthanasia, I thought of the feisty little black and white kitten mewing loudly outside my Southside apartment window. The kitten that I swore would be mine if I had one more sleepless night. The kitten that would eventually follow me home and become my family. Now, holding her as the doctor pushed the medicine filled syringe, I bawled as Sox took her last breaths.

INTIMACY VERSUS ISOLATION

It was quiet in my home. I sat at my desk in front of a black computer screen. For the first time in over a decade, my home did not contain the pitter patter of padded paws. For weeks following Sox's death, Scrappy searched the condo insisting that Sox appear from whatever hiding place she was in. After every unfruitful hunt, Scrappy became more depressed. I went back and forth to the veterinarian's office, but after several visits that failed to answer questions, I knew my dog's depleted energy and dwindling appetite was because he lost his best friend and playmate. I knew that feeling well. Helplessly, I attempted to brighten Scrappy's disposition. With increasing demands at work, I feared I would come home to another dead pet and was heartbroken for my emotionally distressed dog. I decided that Scrappy needed more attention than I had to give. Guilt ridden and with a heavy heart, I put him up for adoption.

Emotionally raw with eyes red and puffy, I sat in my office chair staring out at the fog, the Chicago skyline barely visible through the grey clouds. Cooler days were quickly approaching and the thought of a long, brutal winter in Chicago did not help my somber mood. I decided to drown my sorrows in work, but so far, my administration day had been spent gazing out the window while still wearing my pajamas. I willed my body into action and pushed the computer's power button.

It was nearing the end of the year which meant physician recertifications. It was a time for online training in workplace sensitivity, age-appropriate care, and department specific education. As medical director of the department of obstetrics and gynecology, I was responsible for ensuring compliance among my team. With a lump of loss in my throat, I opened Microsoft Outlook and drafted memos to the doctors comprising my team. I alerted them of their required recertifications and deadlines, and as I pressed send, I heard the chime of incoming mail. The message was from a source external to the hospital system; however, the sender's name was familiar. The subject read

Doc is this your dog?

I opened the email. The sender was one of my patients. She explained that she worked at the pet adoption agency. She reviewed Scrappy's profile, saw my name, and took a personal interest in ensuring he went to a good home. She wanted to let me know that Scrappy was adopted, and she thought it was a perfect match. Fresh tears filled my eyes as I composed a reply expressing my gratitude. I deeply appreciated the email and her message brought relief from the feelings of guilt.

The news of Scrappy's adoption lessened the lump in my throat. I completed correspondence with my team and then turned my attention to my own recertification requirements. I navigated the hospital's intranet and clicked the link to the physician education portal. After entering my credentials, I was granted access to the online learning portfolio. I scrolled through the exhaustive list of objectives and was thankful I gave my team ample notice. Although recertifications were a yearly exercise, it was laborious, and no one looked forward to completing the time-consuming task.

Administering Age-Appropriate Healthcare was first on the alphabetized list. With similar learning objectives annually, the title was familiar, and I recalled that this module was not as grueling as some of the others. Deciding to start there, I pressed the play icon next to the title. The lesson began with an overview of Erik Erikson's stages of psychosocial development. Intrigued by psychology, I perked up as I listened, the information refreshing the knowledge I already had on the subject. Erik Erikson's theory postulates that there are periods of conflict across a person's lifespan. One either resolves the conflict progressing on to the next stage or fails and does not develop the skills necessary to continue along the path to mastery of self. After making bullet points of the eight-stages in Erikson's theory, the module titled *Administering Age-Appropriate Healthcare* announced its focus for the year: Stage Six; Young Adulthood, and the conflict: Intimacy versus Isolation. The lesson continued, defining both intimacy and isolation, and explaining that the goal of this stage of life, ranging from age nineteen to forty, was romantic love. Erikson believed that developing committed loving relationships was vital to psychosocial development and failing at this stage would ultimately result in isolation. The module's lesson was hitting close to home, and I shifted uncomfortably in my chair. My thoughts soon drifted away from the animated lecture on my computer screen.

Finding romantic love was proving to be a challenge for me. It had been a year since the breakup with Kevin, and since then I dated in fits and starts. My conflict was that while romantic partnership was something I thought I wanted, I found the entire process of dating exhausting. Friends suggested I used dating sites, for the ease and convenience. I found nothing easy or convenient about sorting through masses of messages from people who obviously had not read my profile. Finding the open messaging feature overwhelming, I focused my attention on apps that only allowed chats via mutual match. I swiped purposefully, my choices a combination of suspected compatibility and physical attraction. I made matches and went on dates, but they felt orchestrated. I was bored with the repetition of introductory conversation and usually lost interest before making a leap from cute profile to emotional connection.

I hated how manufactured my pursuit for companionship had become and longed to meet someone in the spontaneous whirlwind of life. I wanted to feel the magnetic pull of lust and intrigue created by a chance encounter. I wanted to feel the sensation of disrupted rational thought and irresistible interest. I oftentimes longed for the days when I dated for sport, but lust doesn't lead to love. I was constantly reminded of the perception that engaging in intercourse "too quickly" meant that I would not be taken seriously. I was told about ninety-day rules and other dating dos and don'ts. I attempted to continue dating when there was not instant chemistry, but I found myself disinterested when there were no sparks.

Although moments of intense flirtation and sex were exciting, when it came to becoming a part of my life, I approached intimacy slowly and analytically. Being emotionally vulnerable was difficult, and it took time for me to feel safe enough with someone to share my softer side. Because I approached intimate relationships carefully, I was perceived as cold and aloof. Oftentimes suitors did not think I was interested when I was. I used rationale when dating. I compartmentalized people and conducted emotional risk assessments. Suitors became a list of pros and cons, possible outcomes, risks, and benefits. I moved them closer to the inner circle when they proved worthy, or they were kicked out completely when their actions warranted removal. Aware of the perception that I can be "harsh", if I was interested, I verbalized my feelings and acted accordingly. I made myself available for dates and calls, and initiated interactions, but was continuously perceived as indifferent. My words and actions were not convincing enough to continue courtship. Lacking an understanding of what more was expected of me, the buds of relationships were not allowed to bloom.

Dating left me feeling like a puppy, bouncing up and down in a box hoping for someone to like me enough to pick me. My suitors perceived me to be the runt of the litter. Secondary to my carefree nature, I was "the fun girl", too free spirited to want anything serious. Being outspoken made me "intimidating" and "too direct". I was not soft enough. My career meant that I was too busy. Open communication about sex made me "too sexual" and "too assertive". It was tedious and tiresome, and after a flurry of dates failed to lead to potential partnership, I became exasperated and logged out of the dating scene. Focusing on finding a partner was like clipping my cat's nails, done out of obligation, but far from enjoyable. I was not having fun and receiving advice on the type of woman I needed to become to get a man left me irritated and angry.

As the voice continued to drone in the background, the Grays in my life came to mind. My relationships with those men were not created by an algorithmic match making application. Each of my undefinable relationships spawned from instant attraction and compatible energies. The stories of how I met each of them made our lasting friendships special. Initially, our interactions existed solely in the vacuum of the moments we shared together. With time, genuine friendships developed, and I was closer to the Grays than any of the men I dated in a traditional sense. Having explored the physical attraction free from the expectations of dating sparked a deeper curiosity about them as individuals. We shared our ambitions, hopes, and dreams. We developed comfortable communication and conversed about everything from love to loss. Although my relationships with these men lacked the components of traditional romantic partnerships, they were rooted in mutual respect and genuine friendship. The Grays were a source of comfort, fulfilling my sexual desires and the void of isolation all without the unsettling sense of waiting to be chosen.

"Only five more years for me then, huh? Gee, thanks Erikson." I said aloud only half listening to the lecture coming from my computer. The sadness that had resided in my chest at the start of the day had morphed into a feeling altogether different and an emptiness settled within me; I was lonely. I was no stranger to being single and being alone was usually a safe and happy place. Confused by my uneasiness, I rubbed my forehead in discontent. My mood made for questionable productivity and I logged out of the physician education portal. I checked my phone and had a text from Allen.

Hey! What are you doing for New Year's?

I replied to Allen's message.

No plans yet, but I am off though. What's up?

I had been so busy with work; I had barely given the upcoming holiday season any consideration. New Year's Eve was my favorite holiday, and an ongoing bucket list item was to celebrate in a different city each year. I loved the energy surrounding counting down to a new year. The lights, the fireworks, the music, and people celebrating a spirit of renewal filled me with joy. The countdown was cathartic, and I used the beginning of each year as a time to reflect on years past and set intentions for the next.

Can you talk?

Allen replied to my message, and I picked up the phone and called my grey area friend of almost a decade. Not only was Allen a Gray, but he was one of my closest friends. We saw the world through similar lenses and did not buy into the stereotypes we were force fed daily.

Allen and I met during a night of partying in Orlando, Florida. It was AllStar Weekend, and I was at a club with a male acquaintance, who I had moved into the friend zone the night before. Wearing fitted high waisted black jeans, a cropped, off the shoulder white tee with the words "Why Not" written in bold letters across the front, and spiked toe combat boots, I stood at the bar sipping gin and soda while dancing to the music.

Allen approached the bar and started chatting with other patrons in the area.

"How do you know Emily?" He turned and asked me.

"I don't know Emily." I responded, still dancing, and speaking loudly over the music.

"Oh! I thought you were standing here with, never mind. I'm Allen."

"I'm Rosalyn!"

"Let's go to the dance floor."

We moved onto the dance floor and the natural chemistry between us skyrocketed. I found Allen sexy with his naturally narrowed eyes and full lips. He moved like someone who was comfortable in their own skin and who had a passion for life similar to my own. He matched my energy on the dance floor, and I knew we were kindred spirits. We left the bar together and upon arriving to my hotel, we explored the depths of our physical attraction. After the intimate encounter, we lay in bed hot and sticky and stayed up all night discussing life and travel. We did not say goodbye until the sun shone through the windows.

"Sup Doctor." Allen answered. His speaking voice was a mix of D.C. swag and Atlanta flavor all wrapped up in a bow of education. I smiled every time we spoke.

"Hey friend!" I said with genuine excitement.

"So, about New Years, it is also my birthday week, and I am heading to Tulum and Cancun."

"Sounds like fun! Is this a group trip or are you going solo?"

"I also told some family and close friends, but they got kids and you know how that goes. If they come, they come."

"You know I'm down! Give me the dates and the hotel information."

"That is why your are awesome Doc, always up for anything! I figured we could check out some ruins and cenotes in Tulum and of course party in Cancun."

"Sounds like a great way to start the new year and celebrate your birthday!"

"Bet. I will email you the information. What else is new though?"

I told him about Sox and Scrappy, whom he had met on his visits to Chicago, and he offered condolences. I then told him about the heaviness in my chest and how lonely it was without my pets.

"Damn, Sox was the coolest."

"Wasn't she though!" I exclaimed, and then turning somber I added,

"I miss my cat."

"Get a kitten." Allen offered.

"I am not ready yet. I can usually reflect on something, write about it, and keep it moving, but I dunno." My voice trailed and then I continued. "Adding insult to injury, I just completed a module about a psychosocial theory that basically told me that I am failing at life."

Allen laughed. He always did when I was being dramatic, regardless of the subject matter.

"If you are failing, what does that mean for the rest of us?" He asked.

Now it was my turn to laugh. "Thanks for that." I responded.

"Doc, it is ok to be sad sometimes, you are human, no matter how much you want to be a cat." I laughed heartily.

"You know me so well. Thanks for the reminder Allen."

"Anytime Doc. I got a question for you."

"What's up?" I asked.

"Do you think we will still be friends once one of us gets into a longterm relationship?"

I considered his question. I had lost male friends both platonic and otherwise because of their partners' discomfort. I understood the notion that men and women could not have platonic relationships, but having a male best friend, I disagreed with the sentiment. I answered his question thoughtfully.

"The person that is for me will know who I am through and

through and everything that comes along with me. They will know that I have colored outside the lines and some of my most valued relationships are a product of that. So short answer, yes, we will still be friends."

"I think so too. You're a part of my apocalypse tribe." Allen responded.

I laughed. He reminded me about the dates of the trip and the email outlining the details. We said our goodbyes. Although I was still alone in my condo on a gloomy day in Chicago, I was now excited about the new travel plans and I did not feel lonely at all.

16

THE LONGEST ONE NIGHT STAND EVER

Bursting into my room at the LeBlanc resort, I threw my carry-on on the bed, ripped it open, and pulled out clothing better suited for a night of partying in Cancun. I could not wait to get out of my clothes, shower, and unwind. The last few months had been stressful. Obtaining compliance from a few of the doctors on my team was like wrangling angry cats as I persistently demanded the completion of hospital and state mandated requirements. Finally, under threat of suspension, the documents and certifications miraculously found themselves in my inbox. I rolled my eyes and undressed kicking the clothes into a pile under the bathroom sink. I hopped in the shower and got ready for the party.

Braless in a dark grey racer-back tank with a spider's web laser cut into the back and fitted distressed jean shorts, I put on my black flat chunky sole gladiator sandals and headed out to meet Allen. The atmosphere at Mandala Beach Club was just what the doctor ordered. The bass heavy house music rattled the water in the pool occupying the outdoor nightclub's foreground. Waitresses in iridescent crop tops and shorts carried black buckets containing alcohol and bottle sparklers. The crowd, while not overwhelming in numbers, made up for it with energy and everyone was either splashing around in the pool or on the dance floor. We found a great spot between the pool and the dance floor and a waitress approached us for drink orders. We opted for the open bar option, it was New Year's Eve, and we were going to party all night. Allen and I discovered our natural rhythm together when we met ten years prior, and it did not take us long to get out there and join the quickly expanding crowd on the dance floor. I was dripping with sweat by the time the countdown to the new year was underway. The crowd had thickened, and I could barely hear my own voice as I screamed "Five, four, three, two, one, Happy New Year!" Allen and I embraced each other yelling "Happy New Year!" We then went back to dancing and did not leave until the sun was coming up.

I awoke early the next afternoon to the phone ringing in my hotel room. The sun blared through the open window and I squinted as I looked at the clock and reached for the phone.

"Hello?" I answered groggily.

"Get your ass out of bed!" Allen laughed into my ear.

"Ok, ok, I'm awake." I said still half asleep.

"I got us a beach bed. It's close to the water, meet me there when you get it together."

I hung up the phone and got out of bed.

It was a beautiful day. The sun was beaming, and there was a nice breeze coming off the Caribbean Sea. The rhythmic sound of the waves as they crashed against the sand was soothing as I strolled along the wood planked terrace that ended at the beach. I took off my copper colored flip flops as I approached the plank's end. The sand was warm on my feet and as I walked, my sheer cream sarong blew behind me exposing the olive snakeskin one-piece swimsuit underneath. As I came to the first row of white canopied beach beds, their matching curtains tied to the posts, I looked for Allen.

A waiter was at the daybed when I found the right one. I was starving and the alcohol from last night was begging to be soaked up with carbs.

"Perfect timing." Allen said when he noticed me approaching.

"Yes!" I hissed dramatically. I greeted the waiter and took a spot on the daybed dropping my taupe oversize knit beach bag beside me. I ordered coffee and perused the menu.

"You have a good time last night?" Allen asked.

"I had a blast! You?"

"Yeah. It was fun."

The waiter returned with my coffee and a small side table. I ordered a grilled chicken panini and fries. Allen ordered a burger. During our meals we caught up on work. He filled me in on his promotion at the IT company and talked about new certifications he was interested in picking up. I congratulated him on his accomplishments and filled him in on my time as medical director and department chair. Our conversation had transitioned to dating as the waiter returned at took away our plates.

"So, what happened to that guy you were dating?" Allen asked.

"Shit, which one?" I snorted.

"The one you were so compatible with. Didn't y'all go to Italy?" Allen clarified with a chuckle.

I felt a slight pang and groaned a little. The fiasco in Italy was still fresh in my mind and I recounted the events with colorful accuracy.

After ending my tale, I shook my head and sighed loudly.

"The thing is we had so much in common." I said, still bewildered by the relationship's hard left turn. "I mean he was young, professional, fun, did not want kids, wasn't religious, and wasn't tripping about me cooking or otherwise being domestic. But sassy is what did it."

"You? Sassy?" Allen said, using air quotes when he said the word sassy. Then he added, "Never!" and feigned shock.

"I know, right?" I said laughing. "He called me and wanted to come to Chicago months after."

"What happened?"

"I told him he could say whatever he needed to say on the phone and since he couldn't tell me in person, he didn't say anything."

"He definitely was not expecting you to decline his offer."

"I don't understand why he needed to fly to Chicago for a conversation. We could have just said whatever on the phone and been done with it."

"But that's the point. He thought coming to Chicago would sway you away from being done with it".

"He told me not accepting his offer was all he needed to know. By then it was about more than a grand apology and a trip. He completely shut me out over "the way I say things". I am not going to willingly sign up to be with someone who abandons me during a rocky time."

"He was being manipulative. You were supposed to soften your tone and then be rewarded with his affection."

"Exactly." I said definitively. "He proved just that with his weak ass attempt to coddle me when he saw tears. Ugh."

The waiter returned, and we ordered drinks. Our libations arrived and Allen told me about his dating life and most recent breakup. I listened as he described his feelings of betrayal and manipulation.

"That sucks Allen." I shrugged and lay back on the pillowed daybed. "I am sick of it all to be honest. Dating in general is trash."

Allen told me that he remained hopeful and described his continued search for love in D.C. He told me of mixers and speed dating events, and I envied the energy of his efforts. Although, no promising matches had been made, I applauded him for his continued quest for companionship.

"Dating has for real taken the wind out of my sails. I don't even want to be touched right now." I said, simultaneously discovering and expressing my muted sexual energy. I was not even interested in a vacation romp with Allen, and our natural rhythm extended well beyond the dance floor.

"Damn Doc, that is not like you." Allen said, genuine concern on his face.

"I know! My tingle is gone." I added with a whine.

"You will get your energy back. Maybe this trip will help." Allen said in a reassuring tone.

We lay on the daybed and watched the waves. After a few moments of silence Allen added, "I can see how dating is not fun for you."

"Gee thanks buddy." I returned sarcastically.

Allen laughed. "I am just saying. It is conditioning. You grow up hearing what to want in a woman. So, when someone falls outside of what they have learned to want in a partner, people are going to stray away, or try to make you conform."

I considered his words as I looked out at the sea. Conversations like this one were part of the reason I was so fond of Allen. We were open with one another and he always gave me something to think about.

"Conditioning?" I said questioningly as I thought about my childhood and my relationship with my mother.

"Yep."

"That definitely makes me consider what I have learned consciously or subconsciously along the way."

"We all are a product of our life experiences." Allen said as he pulled out a cigar and torch lighter from his bag.

"In that case I am thankful for the experiences, even the shitty ones. I love this product." I said, popping a pretend collar and reciting lyrics to Megan Trainor's *Me Too*. Allen laughed.

"As you should be. Being you is what makes you awesome, but it also contributes to your issues with dating." Allen said candidly.

"Welp. I guess I will just throw in the towel now then. Sheesh! I really am a cat lady." I said only half joking. We both laughed.

"With all the shit you tell me about you could write a book." Allen stated.

"I have always said I would write a book one day."

Confessions of a Cat Lady." Allen said, puffing his cigar.

"Confessions? Nah, I don't feel the need to be absolved of anything." I retorted. "Tales of a Future Cat Lady is more like it."

Allen nodded in agreement.

The lazy day at the beach morphed into a night seaside party. As the DJ played Martin Solveig and GTA's *Intoxicated*, I was drunk on the notion of writing, and ideas whirred in my mind.

The next day Allen and I toured Mayan ruins on a day trip to Chichen Itza. Exhausted from a late night of partying, we both slept as the tour bus bounced along the Mexico streets. We entered the ruined ancient Mayan city and met our guide. The tour was amazing, and the guide was dynamic as he told stories of the serpent deity Kukulkan. He described the detailed accounts of human sacrifice while the people worshipped at the base of Chichen Itza. The guide spoke of how astrology was used to strengthen the cults hold on the Mayan people and described how the sun slithered down the side of the building during the Equinox appearing to bring the serpent deity to life. We then walked to the Sacred Cenote and stopped to take closer looks at the etchings in the stone ruins along the way. The guide continued his stories and the crowd made faces of disgust as he detailed accounts of bodies deposited there as sacrifices to the rain god. After walking around a few more cenotes, we ended our Yucatan day trip at Museo Del Tequila Don Tadeo. We learned about the tequila making process and sampled a few. A peanut butter infused tequila was my favorite and I bought a bottle. Inebriated from our sampling, we again slept as the bus took us back to the hotel.

"I know what will help get your tingle back." Allen stated boldly after we reconvened for late night fun in Cancun.

"Oh yeah?" I asked curiously.

"I got you Doc." Allen said.

We went to the lobby of LeBlanc and after speaking with the concierge, Allen and I hopped in a cab. We arrived at our destination; Dassan Black Palace. Reminded of a wild night Allen and I shared in Chicago, I cackled with delight as we walked to the entrance of the exotic dance club.

The atmosphere was naughty with red décor and mirrored walls. The dancers were gorgeous and talented, and the staff was attentive. We tipped generously and the party like atmosphere was sensual and exhilarating. One of the dancers, Alegra, was our favorite. She slinked through the club controlled and catlike. She was captivating and when she moved, she too seemed enthralled by her own wiles. Noticing our gaze, Alegra invited us into the Champagne Room. We entered the mirrored space with its black leather sofa and oversized lounge chair. Alegra poured Champagne and then started to dance. Teasing and enticing, she moved under the purple neon lights with raw energy and passion. She was attentive and deliberate, and I enjoyed every minute of her gyrating body pressed against my own. In that moment, I was reminded of my own sexuality and smiled when I felt my tingle return.

The next few days passed quickly, and we were both partied out when we checked out of the hotel on our last day in Mexico. Nursing hangovers at the outside hotel bar, we both laughed at the state we were in. "Thank you for thinking of me. This was a really fun trip." I said.

"Thank you for coming." Allen replied.

"Thank you for listening. I was in a weird place when I got here. I appreciate our talks. And drumroll please." I said tapping my index fingers rapidly on the bar. "I got my tingle back." I said giggling.

Allen laughed. "I'm glad you are feeling better. Listen Doc, sex or no sex, I value you and our friendship."

"Aww. You are my friend for real." I replied in a voice several octaves higher than my natural one and pretended to wipe tears from my eyes.

"I told you, you are a part of my tribe. We are doing Ghana next year."

"Yes!" I agreed excitedly.

Minutes later, his shuttle arrived. We hugged.

"I had a great time." Allen said. "You know this is the longest one-night stand ever, right?" It was a running joke between us, and genuine laughter escaped my lips. We said our goodbyes.

"Write that book!" Allen yelled from the shuttle as he closed the door.

CURIOSITY AND THE CAT LADY TROPE

I returned to Chicago and immediately got back to work. Over the next several months, my clinical practice was busy, and hospital calls were filled with delivering babies and managing emergencies. I felt great about my role as a clinician, however my path as medical director had become rocky. There had been several changes at the hospital administration level. The Chief Medical Officer and nursing manager I began my administrative journey with were replaced and a larger entity had acquired the small Southside hospital. I attended meetings about organizational restructuring and watched as the goals I had for growing my department crumbled. Sitting at my home office desk I rolled my eyes as I read another email about budget cuts and how my departmental initiatives were bold and creative, but nonessential.

My thoughts drifted away from workplace woes and I thought about the conversation I had while on the beach in Mexico with Allen months before. Writing Tales of a Future Cat Lady had been fluttering around in my mind since the idea's inception and had ignited a curiosity that was a welcomed distraction from work. I logged off the hospital system and opened my Google browser. I thought of the seemingly prophetic medical school message to myself. Living life without a romantic partner seemed more probable by the day. The idea no longer invoked fear and seeking out this elusive idea of love had become exhausting. I stared at the screen and remembered someone telling me I would likely die alone surrounded by cats. I snickered and typed cat lady trope into the Google search text box.

The crazy cat lady was a character everywhere. She could be found in comic strips, advertising, anti-suffrage propaganda, and video games. From books to television and movies, spanning all genres, there was sure to be a disheveled spinster surrounded by cats spewing garbled verbiage. Some of the clips I watched were hilarious, but besides having cats, I did not have much in common with the character. A few more clicks navigated me away from pop culture to the historical inception of the cat lady. I was taken to a medieval world of "evil" women and their feline companions. Perceived as witches, these women were believed to be swindlers actively seeking to lure men into their lascivious clutches. One of the first women executed for witchcraft owned a cat, and since that time cats have been linked with the concept of "feminine evil".

After this medieval period, women and cats continued to be characterized together. Women were assigned unattractive cat characteristics such as unapproachable, moody, and fickle. Women with cats were perceived as neurotic and considered just as unmalleable and unaccommodating as their pets. Over time, the stereotype morphed. Crazy replaced evil, and the cat lady became the pitiable, single, sexless, unhinged hoarder of cats.

I shook my head as I read and remembered the cats I had throughout life. My cats had been more than the collection of traits used to marginalize women. My cats had been inquisitive, vigilant, intelligent, and independent. Like Rosalyn and RP, they differed in their degrees of friendliness from the most affectionate Sox to the surly Siegfried. Cats were constant companions during my life's journey and sharing characteristics with them was not a disheartening thought. Cats had saved me from the depths of depression, and I was thankful the universe put me on the path to finding them all those years ago.

Days after Daddy's death, I was aimlessly wandering my Memphis neighborhood streets with fresh tears in my eyes when I heard the muffled cries. I wiped my face and focused on the directionality of the sound. The cries became louder as I approached a fence lined with boards and boxes. Carefully pushing them aside, I gasped in surprise as I uncovered a box containing four kittens. I looked around, there was no other cat or person in sight.

"Oh no, why are y'all out here by yourselves?" I said aloud. I was not speaking much, and my words sounded weak and foreign.

I kneeled to get a closer look. The kittens were orange and white, and I could not tell how old they were, but I figured a few weeks. They cuddled together and whimpered as I knelt beside the box. The kittens were just as alone as I was, and as they cried in the box, I was overcome with the desire to take care of them. I picked up the box of kittens and carried it home. For the first time since my father's death, there was a break in my grief. I walked quickly up the drive leading to my home and into the garage. I placed the box of kittens on the ground and hurriedly opened the garage closet. It was a deep closet used for storage, and I knew the kittens would go unnoticed there. I put them in the closet and quickly made provisions. I got a bowl and filled it with milk, and I took an empty box and made a makeshift litter using potting soil. The cats seemed to perk up and their whimpers turned to purrs.

"I'll take good care of you." I said aloud to my new furry friends.

At first, my kitten companions went unnoticed, but as time

passed the kittens became more active and the closet door was no longer enough to muffle their maturing meows.

"Rosalyn Patrice!" My mother's voice boomed through the house and I knew instantly the cat was out of the bag. I walked towards her voice and before reaching the garage, I was already trembling with fear. "Yes, Momma?" I asked, my voice small and shaky.

She was standing in the garage at the door to my kitten closet, her look stern and eyes squinted.

"Who told you that you could bring those things into my house?" She growled.

"Momma, I—" She cut me off before I could answer.

"I am getting rid of those cats first thing in the morning and taking them to the shelter." Her words dug into me like claws.

"Momma!" I shrieked. "Please momma! Please let me keep them!" I wailed and the pain in my chest made every word a struggle.

My mother stood watching me silently as I tried to talk through my tears. The words "Momma" and "please" were the only ones intelligible through my sobs. Without a word, she brushed past me and towards the door leading back to our home. I watched her, my body trembling and eyes pleading.

Without looking in my direction, she spoke.

"You can keep two of them." She said, disappeared into the house and slammed the door. I crumpled onto the cold concrete and cried.

I barely slept that night. The next morning, I trotted downstairs and into the garage. Knots were forming in my stomach as I opened the closet door. I was relieved to find that there were still two kittens in the closet. I was surprised to see that the makeshift litter-box had been replaced with a real litter-box, cat litter, and a scooper. There was also cat food and new bowls. I shrieked with excitement knowing that the kittens' place in my home was now permanent. I closed the door and sat down cross-legged on the closet floor. I watched the girl kitten; her puffy orange coat seemed to obscure her eyes as she climbed the shelves creating an obstacle course with the items contained on them. The boy kitten cautiously sniffed around and tentatively pawed at my bare toes. I smiled and named my kittens. Frisky Frizz and Kitt the Curious were now officially a part of my family.

I smiled remembering my first cats and thought about all the cats I had since. They all came into my life at the right moments and had provided companionship and comfort. If I had to choose between cats and dating, I would choose cats. I laughed aloud at the thought. I continued to scroll through articles about the cat lady and modern dating, and noticed the implications mirrored those from Erikson's theory on intimacy versus isolation. I shifted my attention to conditioning and socialization. Allen's observation on why dating was not fun for me had made an impression. I pondered the idea that I was devalued as a potential partner because I did not fit into socialized gender norms. Am I an amalgam of all things opposite of what traditional conditioning says I should be? Could my collection of characteristics preclude life partnership? I typed gender socialization into the search engine.

I went down a fascinating rabbit hole on gender stereotypes and socialized gender expectations. I read article after article devouring the information. I found there were socialized gender expectations for everything from domestic duties and libido to religion and sources of comfort. Men have always referred to me as different and according to my research I was not expected to be the woman that I had become. I lacked traits like passivity and the tendency to self-sacrifice. I was not sensitive and was more likely to use rationale than emotion. My disinterest in motherhood was the ultimate distinction. I was indeed not the woman my suitors were conditioned to look for.

"Yikes!" I said aloud. I raised my eyebrows and updated my search to gender stereotypes and dating. I was surprised to find a well-researched topic. According to several articles, the further from traditional gender expectations your characteristics were, the more likely you are to feel stigmatized in romantic relationships. The perception that one differed from traditional gender stereotypes was closely related to feeling less intimate and less invested in those relationships. As I read, I recalled the criticisms of my suitors. My disinterest in dating was causally related to the sense of being stigmatized. I was exhilarated by the collision of theory and real life. I immersed myself in the research and was comforted by stories of shared experiences. Some articles mentioned dating hardships led women to downplay their so-called masculine characteristics to be perceived as approachable, vulnerable, and more feminine. I thought of Kevin and Italy. I thought of the unspoken expectation that I was to diminish myself so that he could feel valuable. In that moment, my research from the cat lady trope to gender norms culminated in one illuminating thought. I am not willing to sacrifice my authenticity for companionship.

I closed my computer and sauntered into the living area, tossing around the new information in my mind. My curiosity had deepened, but the answers I now needed would not be found in Google. To tell my story, I would have to untangle the threads of my life that led to today. I would have to uncover the influences and the choices that charted me along my specific path. Deciding to take a break from my thoughts, I sat down on my couch and grabbed my remote.

I turned on Netflix and tuned in to *Queer Eye*. As the women on the screen described why they nominated their mother for the makeover show, I thought about my own mother. My mother and I are not close, and it had been months since we last spoke.

Conversations with my mother were usually a quick exchange of pleasantries followed by brief rundowns of mundane life events. I rarely confided in my mother about anything of import. If I shared an intimate detail of my life, it was long after any emotion attached to the event had faded into objectivity. I learned long ago my mother was not one for emotional displays of weakness. Any time that fact slipped my mind, I was swiftly reminded of her intolerance. As years passed, we became distant relatives, out of sight and out of mind. Our mother daughter relationship was vastly different from the one of open love and affection displayed on my television screen. In addition to the death of my father, growing up with Momma was another of my life's biggest influences.

18

TIGER MOM

My stomach was in knots as I left Discovery Zone. Yes, I had defended myself, but I knew whatever information the manager relayed to my mother would be what happened. I walked slowly from the recreational arena to my red Pontiac Sunfire coupe. My mother had gotten the car for me when I turned sixteen. After past attempts to persuade my mother to buy a car, I spent evenings and weekends working at Red Lobster to finance my pursuits. I was stunned when we got to the dealership and she told me it was mine. A departure from our usual exchanges, the unexpected act left me speechless.

Before exiting Discovery Zone, I overheard the words "assault" and "pressing charges", but the waves of nausea I felt were not secondary to the looming threat of juvenile detention. The manager had called my mother and she was scarier than thoughts of jail time. My mother lashed out at me unprovoked, so assault charges would be more than enough to incite her rage. I knew she would not show interest in my side or the story, nor would she ask about my physical or emotional well being. My mind raced as I drove at a snail's pace towards my Germantown home. I had learned in my sixteen years that living under my mother's roof was temporary and housing could be revoked at any moment. I was eight years old when I found out the extent of that truth.

I remember watching in anxious silence as my mother grabbed all my sister's belongings and threw them into trash bags. My sister was nineteen and had chosen to get married instead of returning to college. Momma yelled as she stormed down the stairs to the front door.

"As long as you are under my roof you have one job, go to school. If you do not want to go to school, you can be grown somewhere else." Her voice was loud, and its scathing tone was a slap in my sister's face.

My sister tearfully collected the bags from the front door, and I scurried to the window to maintain my view. My sister cried and pled with my mom to let her stay. My mother, impervious to my sister's words, locked the doors and left her outside. I watched my sister as she stood outside in disbelief with tears streaming down her face. When she noticed me watching in the window, she gave me a little wave goodbye and was gone.

I was sweating bullets as I turned into my neighborhood. The spit in my mouth felt thick and worsened the turbulence in my stomach. I pressed the garage opener while silently wishing for the garage to be empty. *Pleas be at work. Please be at work. Plea—*

"Damn. She is not at work yet." I said aloud as I pulled my car into the garage next to hers. Apparently, I had not driven slow enough. I crept into the house and up the stairs. Her bedroom door was closed. *I guess she did not hear me come in.* I thought to myself as Kitt and Frizz mewed. I was sure she could hear their excited meows and was alerted of my return. I shushed my cats, entered my bedroom, and closed the door.

"Rosalyn!" My mother yelled my name moments later.

I opened my door and followed the sound of her voice. She was standing at the bottom of the stairs glaring up at me.

"Yes, Momma?" I asked and sat down at the top of the stairwell. The look on her face warned me not to get too close. Her attire, a button up blouse and pencil skirt, a blazer, and heels, suggested that she was going to work. I was relieved.

"Your job called and told me what you did." She stated. "What the fuck were you thinking? What's wrong with you?" She yelled.

All my mother's questions were rhetorical. Knowing she sought no answers, I remained silent as she continued speaking. She stood at the bottom of the stairs, her slender frame strong and statuesque. With one hand on her hip, she used the other to point at me adding emphasis to her words. Speaking through clenched teeth and in a sharp tone that matched her body language, she said

"I am about to go to work. If the police come get you, take your ass with them. You'll just have to sit there." After reminding me of how worthless I was, Mother stormed out of the house. I cringed at the sound of her heels striking the floor. The tension in my stomach lessened slightly with the sound of her car leaving our home.

I paced. Kitt and Frizz followed me in the circles I walked through my home. I repeatedly ran to the windows and peered out at the sound of any car coming down my street, but there were no police. I ran a bath and as I slid my body into the hot water, tears streamed down my face. I was not sad or ashamed with my actions at Discovery Zone. As far as I was concerned, if the manager had of stopped things with that boy's actions, I would not have had reason to retaliate. I cried because waiting for my punishment was tantamount to torture. I cried because I was alone, and when the police came, I would have to go with them like Momma said. Most of all I cried because my plan had been ruined. The bathroom walls seemed to sway. Suddenly, the warm water was no longer relaxing, but far too hot, and the waves of nausea returned. I scrambled out of the bath and changed clothes. My pulse quickened with anticipation each time I noticed the sound of a car passing by. Darkness approached and I had bitten my nails to bloody nubs, but I continued to wait. There were no lights, no sirens, and no knock at our door. My anxiety gave way to exhaustion and I allowed myself to drift off to sleep.

The garage door opening disrupted my slumber. My mother was back, and her arrival brought back the knots in my stomach. I lay still in my bed and listened quietly, not daring to breathe. I listened to her heels clacking on the floors until they reached the carpeted stairs. Her footsteps were heavy and became louder and louder until they were right outside my door. *Please don't come in.* I thought. I closed my eyes and feigned sleep. I held my breath and listened. The footsteps started again, and the air rushed out of me softening my body when I heard her bedroom door close.

The next morning, I woke to find my car keys had been taken. I knew better than to say anything about it. I was thankful that my things were not packed in garbage bags and I still had a roof over my head. Just as I was getting out of bed, my mother stormed into my room.

"Your little ass got lucky. That boy's momma wanted to send your crazy ass to jail, but that boy is eighteen and he did not want to file a report." She left my room just as suddenly as she had entered. I let out a sigh of relief and sobbed into my hands. Maybe my plan was not ruined after all.

My mother was an authoritarian. Following her rules was mandatory and they were reinforced with punishment. In contrast to the warm, maternal figure ready with sage advice and thoughtful reprimands commonplace on television sitcoms, the earliest memories I have of my mother are laden with her inflicting verbal and corporal punishment. I remember my sisters' wailing in pain after getting in trouble. Unlike my firm yet nurturing authoritative father, punishments from Momma were never followed by hugs or consolatory words. My mother was cold, emotionally unavailable, and did not display physical affection. She never said the words I love you and we did not have chats in the car. My mother gave directives, and I tried hard not to make her angry. I had seen enough of the storm she could reign down, and I wanted to stay out of the way. Inevitably, after my father died and my sisters were gone, I found myself the target of her volatile hostility.

I continued watching the *Queer Eye* mother-daughter relationship, their bond seemingly solidified by makeover magic. I remembered Hawaii, and the last attempt I made to truly bond with my mother. After that trip to Maui, Hawaii, not even the most fabulous of makeovers could repair the rift.

"I'm taking Kyra with me to Hawaii after her high school graduation." My mother announced during one of our rare phone calls.

"Oh nice!" I exclaimed.

"It will be Kyra, my friend, Ruby, and Caren, a girl that works with us."

"I want to come." I stated optimistically. I was pleasantly surprised by my genuine interest.

"Oh! Well in that case get you a plane ticket to Memphis, and I'll get you a pass for the flight to Hawaii." My mother offered. My mother had been and educator and now worked with an airline for fun and travel benefits. Surprised by the gesture, I accepted. My mother and I had been separated by several states for years and this would be the first time we would spend consecutive days together. Although I was nervous about the trip, I hoped that by becoming a doctor, I had finally proven my worth.

It was dark when we arrived in Hawaii. Ruby, my mom, my niece Kyra, and I got to the hotel just before nine. We were right on the beach and the light from the moon illuminated the sand.

"It's so pretty!" Kyra exclaimed. "Let's go outside for a bit Auntie." she said to me.

"Ok let's go!" I replied.

"Kyra, don't let your aunt get you into any trouble out there, you hear?" My mom chimed in glaring at me as she spoke. I had learned to brush off her insensitivities and slighted commentary.

"Thanks Mom." I responded sarcastically. "I'm ready whenever you are Kyra!" I said and turned to my niece unphased by my mother's remarks.

"Kyra, remember what I said, don't let her get you into trouble." My mother repeated.

"Why do you think that I would let anything happen to my eighteen year-old niece? You do realize I get paid to take care of people, right?" I said boldly and shot my mother a look of my own. No longer afraid, I stood staring at my mother until Kyra's voice ended the silence.

"I'm ready, Auntie." Kyra stated. Her excited tone breaking the tension.

I smiled. "Let's go!"

The next day my mother's airline coworker, Caren, joined the group. Caren was around my age and she and I hit it off instantly. Kyra, Caren, and I decided to spend the day at the beach together. Caren was friendly and fun, but I was curious to know more about the relationship she had with my mother. While lying on beach blankets, and enjoying breathtaking views of the Pacific Ocean, I discovered how much Caren loved my mother. I was flabbergasted listening to Caren tell stories of calling my mother for advice. I felt the sting of jealousy burn the back of my eyes as Caren described in vivid detail how my mother has always been there for her. Weeks before the trip, my mother happened to call the same evening I broke up with Carter. She hung up the phone in my face when she heard the sobs in my voice. Feeling exposed and vulnerable as my eyes welled up with tears, I focused my attention on the eye candy walking along the beach.

Over the next several days, we toured Haleakala, the Keanae Arboretum, and went to the Old Lahaina Luau. Each day, I was determined to continue to ignore the jabs my mother consistently threw my way, all while contrasting her behavior towards me to the firsthand account of how close she and Caren were. The final day in Hawaii arrived and I was proud of myself for holding it together. I had wanted this trip to be a bonding experience for me and my mother, however, with the trip coming to an end, we were not any closer and I was anxiously awaiting our departure. We spent one last night in Maui, and with Caren and Ruby gone, it was just family left in the suite. The eye candy I introduced myself to on the beach happened to play for the Na Koa Ikaika Maui, an independent professional baseball team. Kyra and I were going to meet up with our baseball buddies when my mother stopped us in our tracks.

"Where do you think you are going?" She snapped at me.

"I'm going to hang out. There is a party up the street."

"You don't need to go anywhere. That is your problem. You always need to go somewhere." My mother said snidely.

"What is your problem?" I asked, shocked that the words came out of my mouth so forcefully. RP had taken control and I had never spoken to Momma like that before.

My mother appeared shocked as well and since I had her off guard, I took advantage of the rare moment.

"You have been saying little slick shit to me the entire trip. What is that about?" I asked.

"Ain't nobody said nothing to you." She snapped.

"This is why there is no point in having a conversation with you. You refuse to see the things you do and pretend like it is not happening when it is. If you did not want me here, when I asked if I could join, all you had to say was no." I screamed trying desperately not to cry.

"Oh what's that some sort of psychology you learned in medical school. Don't try to diagnose me!" She yelled.

I squinted my eyes and shook my head instead of saying "What the fuck are you talking about lady?" I had decided I was done talking. For a while, I could not take my eyes off her. Just as I was about to turn away, she added, "You are looking at me like you want to beat my ass. Well, come on!"

I scoffed, shook my head, and walked away.

"Raincheck on that party Kyra." I said to my niece before going to my room and closing the door.

I removed my party attire and changed into pajamas. After packing up my things and settling into bed, I lay there thinking about how from the moment we arrived in Hawaii I had been a problem for her. First, there was the implication that I am irresponsible and untrustworthy. Tonight, I am a busy body who wants to beat up her own mother. The heat returned behind my eyes and I allowed the tears to fall. I recalled her interactions with Caren and thought about how differently she treated me and my younger sibling growing up. As the silent tears continued to fall, RP whispered one final thought before I closed my eyes.

"That lady just does not like you Rosalyn, she never has, and she never will."

19

LIFE AFTER DEATH

After my father died, I was gripped in the clutches of grief and the struggle felt like it was mine alone. My mother gave us the news Daddy was gone and there was no further discussion about his life, or his death. She never spoke his name and it was as if he never existed. I had been Daddy's little girl, and I was now left with my affectionless and autocratic mother. Relaxed, loquacious, and giddy with Daddy, I locked myself away with Mother. She and I were strangers, and I had limited memories of bonding with her before Daddy's death. After picking me up from my forced stay with the Retops, my mother never said anything about it. She carried on as if that too, had never happened. Although there would be no explanation for sending me away, I knew. I knew that I had been too sad. It had been months, and while my grief inflicted wounds were not as raw, I still missed Daddy deeply.

Arriving to a new home, being thrown back into a family that had grieved together was strange and unsettling. Watching the sibling and Mother together intensified the sense that I did not belong, and they treated me like an outsider. Their bond was solidified long before heart disease took my best friend. My mother did not play and laugh with me. She watched me; her glaring eyes followed my every move. I was treated like an untrustworthy tenant and I felt like an orphan. She would lurk and stare at me if I were alone for long periods or spent too much time with my cats. My mother never said a word, but I knew what that look meant. I had learned the repercussions of not doing what was expected of you. Fearing a second extended stay at a friend's home, I put on my RP mask and went outside to play with my new Germantown suburb neighbors.

The new neighborhood and new middle school distracted me from my pain and removed me from my mother's gaze. However, even immersed in novelty, I was lonely. After school, I would hop off the bus, let myself into my home, and do my homework. I would play with my cats or write in my journal. The boy who lived across the street, Chris, became my best friend. A tall skinny boy with glasses, he was in my same grade and we had a lot in common. We were both in band and we both liked sports. After school we would meet up and do homework together and then hang out in one of our yards. We made silly jokes and would laugh ourselves into giggle fits over nonsense. I loved being at Chris' house, mostly because his mom was so warm and inviting. Thirsty for affection, her hugs were an oasis in the desert of my childhood.

Filling my days with school, new friends, Kitt, and Frizz, I kept my mind occupied. With RP front and center, I felt better, less sad, and started to connect with the world around me. However, in the darkness of night, my grief returned with a vengeance. I had begun to revisit the night of Daddy's death in my dreams. The ceiling rattling thud, the violent coughing, and Daddy whispering bye, played on repeat night after night. In my nightmares, I would chase the ambulance through the neighborhood screaming "please help". I would run and run. Yelling "please help" repeatedly until the ambulance was lost in the dark. The dream would then start back at the beginning and I would be in my old house watching

Wildcats and waiting for the thud. I would wake up with a tear-streaked face and a wet pillowcase. I would cry into my pillow, not daring to make a peep. While those dreams were distressing, the cause of my bedtime torment was that *the Lady* was back.

Days before my dad died on a night like any other, I got into bed, lay on my back, and pulled the covers under my chin. I placed my arms atop the blanket and relaxed into the soft mattress. Moments after settling into a light sleep, the rustling of layered fabric moving through the halls awakened me. I watched as a dark figure appeared in front of my open door. It stopped and turned to me. The figure wore a long, black dress with a layered full skirt. The width of the garment suggested a petticoat was underneath, and the ruffled lace swayed and whispered as she moved closer. It wore a black veil that hid any facial features and as I lay there frozen and unable to scream, I wondered if it had a face at all. The figure moved slowly into my room, its motion did not have the bounce of a walk and instead seemed to glide towards me. Hovering at the foot of my bed, I watched in terror as its arms reached out towards me lifting my blanket up and away from my body. Tears streamed from my face as the warmth of the blanket was replaced with the cool night air. Hovering above me as I trembled in my bed, it then began to move again and slowly floated backwards into the hallway, turned, and went back the way it came. I could still hear the rustling of the dress as I cried myself back to sleep.

Now *The Lady* had returned and seemed to control the content of my dreams, turning pleasant memories of my father into macabre scenes of horror. Dreams of my dad smiling ear to ear, enjoying one of our rides in the Dodge Daytona would suddenly shift. My dad's smiling face would change, and his features would become distorted. His mouth would drop open, and cockroaches would pour out. I would scream as the army of bugs covered my body; the tiny tapping of legs magnified by the thousand. I would swat them away in futility and frantically try to get out of the car.

The Lady would then appear beyond the windshield hovering and watching as I flailed around in fear. I would force my eyes open becoming aware of my own screams but could not move. Stuck in the night terror, the bugs crawled on my skin. My mother would burst into my room, grab me by my arms, and yell my name.

"Oh Rosalyn! Wake up! Let her go Hag!" Her attempts to shake me awake unsuccessful, I would cry and cry until the roaches were gone and *The Lady* disappeared from my doorway. After I had calmed myself, my mother would leave my room fussing about how "y'all children get on my damn nerves". She never asked what my dreams were about or why I was so afraid. I was to take my ass to sleep as instructed, and that was to be the end of it.

It became harder for me to fall asleep. I would lay there waiting for *The Lady* to show up at my door. I would drift asleep for minutes and jolt awake, expecting the lady in the black dress and veil to be hovering at the foot of my bed. Some nights, I would sneak out of bed and go downstairs to play with Kitt and Frizz and watch television. I would flip through the channels of the cable box in attempts to fill my mind with content far from the nightmares waiting for me in my room.

One late night, I was aimlessly flipping channels when naked bodies on Cinemax caught my attention. Until then, sex was an abstract subject that I had only heard whispers about. It was "doing it". Although I did not know what "it" was exactly, "it" was the reason I giggled when I saw my sisters kiss their boyfriends or husbands. "It" was why "ooh" was yelled by kids when they saw couples displaying affection. "It" was something I knew I was too young for and that I better not do up in my momma's house.

I had stumbled upon the erotic film series *Emmanuelle*. The naked bodies on my screen touched each other in places I had been instructed to always keep covered. I was overcome with curiosity as I watched the movie's sex filled scenes. I sat wide-eyed as the people on the screen became engulfed in pleasure, smashing their private parts against each other. A tickle started to rise in the pit of my stomach, and I let out a quiet, nervous giggle. The tickle became a deep tingle and I started to feel it in an area deeper and lower than my stomach. The longer I watched the more intense the tingling became. I heard a noise upstairs and fearing being found out, I turned off the television and returned to my room. The sense of fear was gone. All I felt was the tingle and I liked it. I got into bed, closed my eyes, and immediately fell asleep. *The Lady* did not make an appearance that night and my dreams were not scary at all.

A few nights later, I was startled awake. I pawed at my face wildly and kicked the bed sheets off my body. The bug nightmare had returned which meant *The Lady* was not far behind. I jumped out of bed and turned on the lights still swiping in futility at bugs that were not there. My racing heart urged me to stay awake. Too afraid to lay back down, I crept down the stairs and turned on the television. I immediately turned to Cinemax and was delighted to again find naked bodies pressing themselves together on the screen. I watched eagerly and awaited the tingle. The sensation returned and my stomach and vagina pulsed with intensity. The sensation was stronger than it had been days before and I clenched my thighs together in response. Overwhelmed, I turned off the television and ran to my room.

I hopped in my bed, lay on my stomach, and pulled the covers over my head. I closed my eyes, but the tingle was still raging. Pressing my pelvis into the bed, my body yearned for something I did not quite understand. I pressed my hips deeper into the bed and began moving in rhythmic motions. The tingle turned into something different, and it felt good. I turned on my back and put my hand into my panties. I had never touched my private parts like that before and I found that I liked the sensations coursing through my body. I thought about Emmanuel and the bodies I had seen on the television screen. I wondered what would happen if –.

The thought sparked a deeper curiosity and I got out of bed and looked around my room. Opening my closet door, I searched my toy box for something small and phallic. Among the puzzles, computerized toys, board games, and barbie dolls, nothing seemed to offer the solution I was looking for. I was just about to go back to bed when I picked up the barbie doll and ripped off its leg. I hopped back into bed and pulled the covers over my head. I slowly guided the barbie leg towards the tingle. The release that followed sent shockwaves through my body. I got to know myself that night and there was no more pain or fear. I tucked the dismantled barbie appendage under my mattress for later use. I fell into the deepest and most restorative sleep that I had gotten since the death of my father and I never had night terrors again. With night terrors a thing of the past, grief loosened its grip and I started to heal. I had learned how to escape the pain in my life by dismantling a doll and discovering self-pleasure.

20

FAST ASS LIL' GIRL

I was eight and in third grade when my youngest elder sister's eviction notice was served. It was a time when boys and girls passed notes in class and hitting one another was a form of flirtation. I was completing the class assignment, a worksheet, pressing pencil to paper when the lead broke. I got up from my desk and walked to the pencil sharpener at the back of the class. As I wound the handle to the wall mounted manual sharpener, a folded piece of paper landed at my feet. I looked around as I removed my newly sharpened No. 2 pencil. Bending down to pick up the paper, I noticed Eddie looking in my direction and smiling. I returned to my desk and unfolded the note.

Do you like me? Yes or No

The words were scribbled across a torn piece of wide ruled notebook paper. I furrowed my brow, crumpled the paper into a ball, and slowly turned to look at Eddie. I glared at him as I punched my right fist into the palm of my left hand. I saw his smile disappear as I turned back around. *Boys will not get me in trouble.* I thought to myself. I picked up my pencil and got back to work.

After I threatened to beat him up for "liking" me, Eddie and I became friends. We played together during recess and always chose to be in the same small groups. I had decided that if I could not like boys, I would be like them. Boys were carefree and fun. They were never crying over girls and girls did not seem to get them "in trouble". I developed a comfort with boys that I lacked with most of my female companions. While my female friends talked about boys, barbies, and clothes, I was a tomboy. I fought with boys and broke down dolls for parts. With boys, I could be my complete self, boisterous, goofy, aggressive, and loud. Like Eddie before him, Chris became my new best friend. Chris' friends became my friends, and soon I was just another one of the guys. My mother would scowl and roll her eyes.

"I don't know why you always have to surround yourself with all of those little boys." She would say. I consistently attempted to reassure her that they were only my friends, but it did not matter. My mother always replied, "Don't be out there being fast."

By the time I was fifteen, my interest in boys was well past friendship. I was not afforded the parental leniency my peers enjoyed and in my early teen years my mother's short leash curtailed my desires for romantic socialization. My mother had made it clear that I was not allowed to date and "being fast" was punishable by exile. I became cleverer in my attempts at independence, and I used time with friends to flex the muscles of flirtation.

I was with Joy at Appletree movie theater when we met Dean and Brenden. Appletree was not just any movie theater, it was a teen hang out spot. On any Friday or Saturday night, there were throngs of teens throughout the building. There would be groups gathered around gaming machines in the lobby and chatting by the concession stands. Joy and I were laughing at my attempts to use a mechanical claw to win a stuffed Tasmanian Devil toy when Dean and Brenden approached us. Brenden was tall with a big bright smile and I smiled back. He joined me at the mechanical claw while Dean and Joy chatted behind us. After helping me win Tax, we exchanged numbers.

For months we talked on the phone and I kept our relationship away from my mother. I turned off the ringers to the second phone line in our home, only alerted to a call by the red indicator light's flashes. Times when I was with Joy, Brenden and I saw each other in person. We would meet up at the theater or East End skating rink, another popular teen hangout. Brenden, Dean, Joy, and I would hang out at his place and his mom adored me. I confided in my sister and she allowed us to hang out at her home after I finished babysitting.

The summer before eleventh grade, I was a hostess at Red Lobster. Brenden and I were still dating, and my mother continued to be in the dark about my first boyfriend. My mother was attending a conference in Georgia for a few days and although I was scheduled to work at Red Lobster, I planned to use my mother's absence as an opportunity to see Brenden. I called Tony, my manager, and told him I could not make it to work. I then called Brenden and we planned our day.

I put on a bright orange, yellow, and green floral print knee length dress. It hugged my slender frame and my budding breasts before fanning out at the waist. Paring it with ballet flats, I felt like a pretty princess. Before leaving the house, I grabbed my work clothes and stuffed them into a bag. My mother was not supposed to arrive home until the following day, but just in case.I had been granted the use of the car and I met Brenden at the movie theater. *FaceOff* was entertaining, and other than intermittent moments of kissing, we watched the entire movie. Afterwards, Brenden and I walked the mall and took pictures together at a Sear's photography studio. After a day of laughter and fun, I drove us back to his place.

Brenden's mother was not home. The kissing and heavy petting that had become commonplace in our relationship started up almost instantly. Brenden's arousal was obvious, and I was curious about the male body. I reached out my hand slowly to touch the firmness that had formed at his crotch. We kissed deeply and our hands explored each other's bodies. "Don't you bring no babies up in my house!" I jumped as my mother's words rang out in my head.

"Why did you stop?" Brenden asked breathlessly. I moved my hands from his body and his from mine.

"I can't." I responded.

Brenden held his swollen member in his hands and stood up. After making a joke about blue balls, he went to the bathroom to "take care of it". Brimming with curiosity, I followed him towards the bathroom and sat on the hallway floor. I watched in amazement as Brenden took care of himself and we both eagerly awaited his climax. A banging on the door startled us, interrupting my show and Brenden's release.

"What the fuck?" I said looking at him questioningly.

"I don't know who that could be." He responded while quickly pulling up and zipping his pants. His little, white dog, Snowflake, rushed past my legs as I stood to my feet. The dog barked loudly at the door as the unknown visitor continued to knock. Still shirtless, Brenden went to the front door and opened it. My eyes widened in terror as I stared at the uninvited guest. Standing on the opposite side of the screen door was my sister. A pit formed in my stomach and my mind started to race. What is she doing here? The silent frantic question repeated in my mind. My knees felt weak as I straightened my disheveled hair and pulled my dress down from being hiked up high on my thighs. Brenden slowly opened the door and as he let my sister inside, Snowflake bolted out of the house and down the street. Brenden gave me a worried look and mouthed "I'm sorry" before chasing after Snowflake.

"Your momma is home and is looking for you." My sister said. "She knows you are not at work."

I quickly gathered my belongings and left the house.

"Does she know where I am?" I asked my sister, my voice full of trepidation.

"She doesn't, but I figured you would be here." My sister said, her tone not at all reassuring. "You need to go home." She added before getting into her car.

My sister followed me home, and with the wrath of my mother waiting for me, I was grateful for her presence. I walked into the house and my mother's reaction was swift and immediate. She stood at the top of the stairs as I walked towards her.

"Give me my goddamn keys." She yelled snatching the keys from my hand. "This is what you do when I leave huh? Dress like a fucking whore. Where were you, Rosalyn?" She asked. Her question felt like a threat. I walked back down a few steps and remained silent. My sister answered for me.

"She was at her boyfriend Brenden's house."

I was not sure how I felt about Linda's candor, but had little time to consider that. My mother erupted.

"Boyfriend? I have told you time and time again, there ain't gonna be no babies in my house!"

"I'm not having sex momma!" I pleaded, tears starting to form at the corners of my eyes.

"You think I believe anything you say? You look like you are out here prostituting yourself." She screamed.

I looked down at my floral print dress. I felt so pretty and girly in it while I was out with Brenden. Now standing in front of my mother, I felt like Cinderella as her creation for the ball was ripped to pieces by her evil stepfamily. I glared at my mother.

"Girl, you better get that look off your face. Out here dressed like you are selling pussy. If you are going to sell your pussy, how about selling it for me and making me some money!"

Her words were venom, and as the poison seeped into my psyche, I could no longer hold back my tears.

"If you don't like it, get the fuck out!" She screamed before going to her room and slamming the door behind her.

My sister and I stood silently in the stairwell.

"Rosalyn, you can stay with me." Linda offered softly as she wrapped her arms around my shoulders.

"Thanks sis, but can you take me to Joy's house instead?"

"Sure." She responded.

I went to my room and changed from the floral print dress to jeans and a t-shirt while my sister waited in the doorway. I put away my whore dress, and as tears continued to flow down my cheeks, my sister spoke softly.

"Rosalyn, you did look pretty in your dress. I don't know why our momma treats us like that."

"Thanks Linda. I'm ready." I responded. I gave my cats belly rubs and left my home.

Joy and I embraced each other, and more tears came streaming down as I told her and her mom about my day.

"You are sixteen years old!" Joy's mom, Paula, said. The shock was apparent in her voice. "Being curious about love and sex is completely natural!" She continued. Paula embraced me and I buried my face in her bosom as tears continued to flow.

"How is your mom and dad's relationship?" Paula asked gently.

"Momma, Rosalyn's daddy died when she was ten." Joy responded in my stead.

"Oh, Rosalyn. I'm so sorry." Paula replied.

I straightened my body and cleared my throat.

"It's ok. I do not mind. I like talking about my daddy and rarely have an opportunity to do so. My parents' relationship seemed great. They had been married for over twenty-five years before Daddy died. I never heard them argue, so if they did, it was not in front of us. He seemed to hold the keys to her crazy and sometimes she even looked happy. Our family felt like a family back then."

The tears returned to my eyes and Paula rubbed my back.

"You can stay with us for as long as you want." Paula said.

"Thanks Mrs. Teal." I replied, wiping tears away from my eyes.

After the great day with Brenden dissolved into disaster, our relationship dissipated. I stayed with Joy for weeks. I received a call from Daphne, another of my older sisters telling me it was ok to come home. She explained that she had spoken to and reasoned with Momma on my behalf. I had anxiety surrounding returning home, so I asked about my cats instead. She told me they were fine and added that she was going to be staying at home with us for a while.

"As long as someone other than the sibling is there with me, I'll come back." I finally answered.

"I got you sis."

Daphne provided a much-needed mother buffer in my home, and her presence afforded me some teen freedoms. Although my mother continued to express her disdain, during the first month of my senior year in high school, I went on my first real date.

JUSTIN WAS EVERYTHING A PARENT COULD WANT FOR A DAUGHTER. Handsome, well-mannered, and intelligent, Justin was also a star athlete. He and I met years before in a Driver's Education class I took with Joy at the Memphis Board of Education. All the girls liked Justin. During attempts to set him up with one of our driver's ed classmates, he asked for my number. Because I was not allowed to date, I was hesitant, but after giving him my mother's phone etiquette rundown, we exchanged numbers. We talked on the phone almost daily and sometimes he would meet Joy and I at East End or Appletree. Justin and I became great friends during those two years, and although we had spent time together on numerous occasions, when Justin rang the doorbell for our first date, I had butterflies.

Justin became my first love and we explored sex for the first time together. Our relationship was special, and we spent a countless amount of time with one another. It was obvious to everyone that we were a happy couple. Alas, my mother did not celebrate our love and made sure that I felt her threatening presence. Justin was not allowed in my room and we could only interact in the common areas of my home. If she saw us together and thought we were too close, she would stand and watch us scowling until either he or I became so uncomfortable, that we would separate. My mother would then walk away, rolling her eyes only to summon me once she reached her room.

"Rosalyn Patrice!" She would roar.

Excusing myself from my company, I would trot upstairs and slowly enter her room and await my admonishment. Glaring at me for what would seem like minutes she would finally speak.

"Look lil' girl, I know you think you grown, but don't be being fast in my house."

I would take her words in silence, only turning to leave when I was sure she was done speaking. As I rejoined Justin downstairs, I thought to myself, almost there, Rosalyn. One more year to go.

21

SCARS

I grabbed my white three-quarter length sleeve cropped jacket from my bedroom closet just as the doorbell rang. I skipped downstairs and excitedly opened the front door. With a large smile and hug, I warmly greeted my boyfriend and first love. I still got butterflies every time I saw Justin. Our hello was interrupted by my mother's voice.

"Rosalyn Patrice!" She yelled from her room. I rolled my eyes.

"I'll be right back." I said to Justin before returning upstairs to answer my mother's call.

"Yes Momma?" I said as I entered her room.

"Where are you going?" She asked while looking me up and down.

The way she looked at me put an unsettling feeling in my stomach.

"I'm going to the movies with Justin." I answered softly. She stared at me in silence. *Why is she looking at me like that?* I wondered silently and moved further into her room. Waiting to be dismissed, I furtively glanced at myself in her dresser mirror. I thought I looked cool and fun in my high waisted denim cropped leggings, a blue and white tie-dyed halter top with a blue butterfly embroidered on the front, and flat blue and white tie-dyed Keds. My hair was in a curly high ponytail and I wore light pink lipgloss, which was the only make up my mother allowed.

Fully dressed and ready for my date, I felt naked as I stood trapped in her gaze. The tiny hairs on my arms stood at attention in response. I rubbed both forearms with my hands. For a moment, my Justin induced excitement disappeared as my hands grazed over the keloids on my skin. My mother finally spoke.

"You are gonna get your ass beat looking like that."

Stunned, I continued to survey my outfit in the mirror. Then I turned to my mother.

"Like what Momma?" I asked confused.

"Nothing. Just go." She said and waved me away. With that, I was dismissed and left her room.

I trotted back down the stairs. As usual, my mother's words had been unkind. However, as I hopped into Justin's blue van, I convinced myself that "you are gonna get your ass beat looking like that" was her way of giving me a compliment.

My mother took pride in her physical appearance. Evident in the way she dressed, my mother never left the house "looking any ole way" and most times her impeccable outfits were paired with heels. Physically fit, my mother exercised nightly, and the rhythmic sounds of her pulley rope door exercise system provided the soundtrack to my evenings at home. My mother demanded that her daughters took that very same pride in their appearances. I heard her say repeatedly that "Porter women did not leave the house looking a mess." "Porter women walk with confidence." If she were displeased with the way we looked or the way we carried ourselves, my mother made us aware of our transgressions.

"GET YOUR ASS ON THE GROUND AND EXERCISE. YOU GOT ME IN here making this dress. Your fat ass won't be able to get in it." My mother yelled at my sister. I was seven, and I watched my sister work hard to be the size my mother deemed appropriate for prom. Night after night, my sister would exercise, coordinating her efforts with the timing of my mother's nightly workout. She dieted and tried to stay upbeat despite my mother's disparaging commentary. On the night of her prom, I thought my sister looked like royalty in her white dress with royal blue laced overlay. As the family gathered to send her on her way, my mom did not say a word. She just watched the scene with that same scowl that I had grown so accustomed to and murmured under her breath.

As a chubby kid with problematic bowel habits, my mother often told me I was going to be "big, tall, and fat, just like your daddy's momma." When I announced my interest in athletics my mother exclaimed "Good! Hopefully, that will keep you from getting as big as a house. Exercise keeps your pussy tight anyway." Now, as a slender teen on my way out on a date, I apparently looked like I was asking for a fight. My mother rarely commented on my appearance and hearing her do so was perplexing.

That was a compliment. I repeated to myself, my internal reassurances more believable this time. Justin and I left for the movie theater, and while my mother's words had not dampened my excitement, they still occupied my mind. Absentmindedly, I traced the keloid on my left arm and reminisced on how it got there.

"Please momma!" I begged, trying not to cry. "I don't want to catch it! Send the sibling to grandma's house like you did when Linda got it!"

The sibling had contracted chickenpox from a classmate. Unlike most kids, the younger sibling and I did not go to day cares or preschool. Having built in babysitters since birth, there was no need for alternative forms of childcare. Therefore, when most kids were mass inoculated with the pox virus, the younger sibling and I were safe in our homes being cared for by our teenage sisters. I was in tenth grade when my mother picked me up from band practice and told me the news. With a band performance, several exams, and a track meet quickly approaching, I did not want to risk getting chickenpox. I pled with my mother the entire car ride home. Initially she remained silent, only the rolling of her eyes alerted me she was listening at all.

"I am not taking your sibling anywhere. If you get it. You get it." She responded as she pulled the car into our garage.

Later that week, I felt ill after track practice. Thinking I had just overexerted myself on the track, I showered, washed my hair, and went to bed early that night. The next morning, I did not feel better, but in my mother's house, you had one job. So, I went to school. I slowly trekked to my first period class. Entering Mr. Shipp's Introduction to Spanish class, I took my seat slowly as I fought off the waves of dizziness. There was an aching in my head and my eyes felt heavy. Today's lesson was the conjugation of the verb comer. As we conjugated the verb which meant to eat in Spanish, I swallowed down the watery acidic taste building in my mouth.

"Repeat after me class. "Yo cómo." Mr. Shipp's voice seemed louder and more abrasive than usual.

"Yo cómo." The class repeated in unison.

My own voice sounded miles away as Mr. Shipp continued the conjugation lesson, "Tu comes."

"Tu comes." The class answered back.

I could hardly concentrate on Mr. Shipp's voice as he said, "El, Ella, Usted come."

My body had begun to tremble. Without warning, the first blister erupted through the skin on my forehead. My surprised gasp was drowned out by the class's repetition of "El, Ella, Usted come". I then felt the skin eruption again. This time, it was in my scalp. Soon the pox forcefully made their way to the surface of my skin in quick succession like popcorn kernels flipping inside out after reaching critical pressure. It was almost as if I could hear the pox bursting through my skin. Mr. Shipp was on the "Ellos, Ellas, Ustedes comen" verb form when I raised my hand.

"Si, Senorita Porter?" Mr. Shipp asked.

In my growing sense of urgency, I could not find the Spanish words to respond.

"Necesito voy—um" I started. As the pox eruptions in my scalp and on my face continued, I blurted out, "I think I have Chickenpox and I need to go home."

Mr. Shipp recoiled. "Really? Aren't you a little old for chickenpox?"

"I have never had them before." I stated.

"Yes, you are excused."

I hurriedly collected my things and briskly walked out of the room as the entire tenth grade Spanish class watched in horror.

Upon arriving home, the pox completely covered my face, scalp, and upper torso. I was unrecognizable with my pox distorted face and my skin was never the same. Despite taking extra care not to scratch, the pox left me with scars. The serpiginous hyperpigmented lesions marred the surface of both of my arms, right shoulder blade, and under my right breast. Long after the pox cleared, the keloids left behind were itchy imperfections that grew larger with each passing day. Prior to having chicken pox, a scratch or wound would heal without a trace. After chicken pox, even the slightest of injuries would leave a keloid in its place. The scars were aesthetically displeasing, and the itching was incessant. I bought creams and tried numerous skin care routines. I tried silicone tapes and over the counter scar fading ointments. I researched scar revision and removal which led me to seek the advice of plastic surgeons and dermatologists. Treatment after treatment failed and the keloids continued their growth. The scar revisions and steroid injections seemed to anger the lesions and they became bigger beefy growths complete with intensified itching. During my first year in medical school, I had another excision of three of the keloids. Following their removal, the skin on my shoulder blade and both arms were radiated which finally ended the excessive scarring in those areas. Given the aggressive therapy, the lesion under my right breast would be left untreated. I hated those scars, and I blamed my mother for my skin's flaws.

When it was time for my senior prom, my plan was to purchase dresses. Justin and I went to different high schools, so I would attend two senior proms. I planned to take on extra hours at Red Lobster to afford the dresses, but my mother insisted on continuing her tradition of making prom dresses for her children. I accompanied my mother to Hancock Fabrics and searched through the aisles of patterns. After settling on two dresses that did not look "too whorish" we returned home so that she could take measurements. I went to my room and undressed.

When my mother came in, tape measure in hand, I felt myself shrink. I had been naked with Justin on numerous occasions and flaunted my body without shame or feeling self-conscious. However, as I stood before my mother in a bra and panties, I was insecure.

"Girl, ain't nobody thinking about nothing you got." She said noticing my discomfort. "Now stand still." She placed the tape measure here and there. She muttered and groaned taking breaks to jot down numbers and abbreviations.

"Turn around and lift your arms up and out."

I did as she instructed. Facing the mirror with my arms outstretched, I watched as my mother wrapped the tape around my chest and back.

"Damn girl. You got a big back. You are wide as hell. I may not have gotten enough fabric." As the insults and derogatory commentary started flowing from her lips, I retreated to the safe inner sanctum I had created in my mind. My mother's insults became distant whispers, and I studied my almost naked body as she continued her measurements.

Standing at five feet eight inches tall with a short torso and high waist, my legs were long and slender, yet muscular. I also had long, muscular arms, toned by years of team sports. My shoulders and back were broad but my proportions were flattering. My hair was past my shoulders, and at the time I wore it in a long bob. My favorite thing about myself was my face; oval-shaped, with full lips, doe-eyes, and a cute little nose in between. I was thankful that although most of the pox had been located on my face, my face was the one place they did not leave scars.

I loved the way I looked and as a senior counting down the days to graduation, I was no longer concerned with my mother's opinion or anyone else's for that matter. RP had grown a thick skin and refused to tolerate anyone's belittling or demeaning words. Focusing on the scars as I continued to hold my position, I fought the urge to look at my mother and roll my eyes.

"Ok girl." My mother's phrase announced the completion of her task. I quickly threw on an oversized T-shirt and watched as she left my room. After years of tears, her opinions about my appearance no longer catapulted me into a depression. That realization brought a small smile to my face. Soon you will be gone for good. I reminded myself, and my small smile became a toothy grin.

22

B'S ARE BAD

With only two months left in high school and an acceptance to Xavier University of Louisiana in hand, I was ecstatic when I learned of the Bill and Melinda Gates Millennium Scholars Program. It was a dream come true. The scholarship would pay for everything from college to medical school and even covered living expenses. This scholarship would ensure that I was leaving home for good. I would not have to ask my mother for anything ever again. I sealed the envelope to my application for the Bill and Melinda Gate's Millennium Scholars Program and kissed it for luck. All my scholastic achievements and never-ending extracurricular activities were about to pay dividends and I would finally be free. I dropped off the envelope at USPS and crossed my fingers.

One of the first things I learned about myself was that I was smart. My mother demanded excellence, and thankfully, excelling in the classroom came easy for me. I grasped concepts quickly and swiftly surpassed students in my peer group. By the time I was ten, I was bussed to the high school for English classes and read to the classes at my elementary school grade levels below my own.

While I enjoyed learning, the most important lesson was not attained in class. I learned that school was my one job. A's were the expectation and my mother did not tolerate mediocrity.

After one such trip to the high school, I entered my Lauderdale Elementary classroom and settled at my desk. As I sat watching my soon to be ex classmates chatting amongst themselves and waiting for class to start, a sense of nostalgia washed over me. There was Bria, the girl who fell apart when her mom dropped her off on our first day of Kindergarten. I comforted her and we became fast friends. Richie was also a part of the gifted program and I would miss making him laugh on the bus. Marcie was quiet and sweet. I still laughed about the day she tripped and fell down the stairs. The bouncing of her short pigtails tied with hair ballies had been funny. It was my last day at Lauderdale Elementary School, and I was thinking of how much I would miss everyone when Ms. Black walked in. I would not miss her. She was harsh and stern and did not like me very much. I did not like her either. She reminded me of my mother, and I refused to have more than one bully in my life. She hated that I did not cower before her. I always looked her directly in her eyes, no matter how demeaning her words. Ms. Black paddled me once for talking back. It pissed her off even more when I did not cry.

"Rosalyn is leaving us you guys." Ms. Black announced at the end of the day. Her smile was plastic and too big to be real. The classes words were murmurs as everyone spoke "aww" and "we'll miss you" simultaneously. The bell rang and I gathered my things. My classmates hugged me as they left, and the pang of change brought the sensation of tears. As the first tear was about to make its way down my cheek, Ms. Black's touch sent chills down my spine. She pulled me close wearing a smile too wide for her face and I shuddered as my body contacted hers. My arms dangled at my sides and I tried not to squirm as she hugged me. She released me from her embrace and placed her hands on my shoulders. She leaned in close and with that grisly grin still spread across her lips she said,

"Germantown's curriculum is extremely challenging. It will be a much more vigorous experience than it is here." She added one more thing before releasing my shoulders and with these words her smile was gone. "You won't make A's there."

I gave her a blank stare, and said in a cheerful tone, "Bye Ms. Black!" I headed out the door and looked back for a moment to give her a huge grin of my own. Ms. Black failed to realize that making A's was the only option in my mother's house.

I continued the straight A streak during my time at Germantown. Ms. Black had been correct, the curriculum was more challenging. The challenge was fun, and I took pride in the ease at which I elevated to the new standard. Report card days became my favorite time. There would be no rewards or praise waiting for me. I had simply met my mother's expectations, but I looked forward to report card day all the same. It was the one day every six weeks when I was almost guaranteed not to be "in trouble".

I tucked my report card into the cover of my tenth-grade literature book as the bell rang at the end of class. I will look at it later. I thought as I filed out of class and looked for my friends in the hallway. Erica and I chatted for a bit too long and the next bell rang sooner than expected. We started to run in opposite directions and collided with one another knocking my literature book to the floor. Erica and I both laughed as she bent over to pick up my book and the report card that had flown from the book's cover. She looked at it.

"Dang girl! Smarty pants!" She spoke as she scanned my grades. "Rosalyn! I did not know your crazy ass was so smart!" I laughed, dramatically snatched my report card from her hands, and ran to class.

I sat in my sixth period English literature class, and as Mrs. Williams outlined the day's assignment, I fought with the twisting in my stomach. I had a *B* on my report card. The room became extremely warm. I closed my eyes and placed my hands on my desk. I took several deep breaths, but the waves of nausea sloshed in my body. I swallowed hard and slowly raised my hand. "Mrs. Williams, I need to be excused."

I rushed out of my seat and flew out of the classroom and into the bathroom across the hall. I pushed open the stall door making it to the toilet just as the vomit erupted from my mouth. After the retching stopped, I cried as I wiped my mouth at the sink. The tears threatened the return of the retching and I tried to compose myself. Mrs. Williams entered the bathroom and the concern on her face led to more tears.

"What's wrong?" Mrs. Williams asked.

"I. I Go- B. On ma- repo- card." I said in broken tearful language.

For a moment, I could not read Mrs. Williams face as she stood close to me her hands resting gently on my quivering shoulders. Her next statement clarified her demeanor.

"Rosalyn, calm yourself. It is ok. *B*'s are not bad." She said, with a bewildered look.

"In my house they are!" I cried with panic in my voice.

Mrs. Williams hugged me and returned to class. I had not even told her the worst part; the *B* was in Algebra 2.

My scholastic perfection had mostly kept things peaceful between my mother and I, and as I rode the bus home that afternoon, I feared the repercussions of my shortcoming. I was constantly instructed to do and learn more. I was even in school on Saturdays. My mother would leave the Saturday Scholars brochure in my room and without instruction, I would look it over and pick a course to take. The options ranged from foreign language to advanced chemistry and everything in between. I did not dare argue about school on a Saturday and the opportunities to learn also got me out of the house. I became proficient at typing and computer literacy. I took classes ranging from

Microsoft Office to advanced biology. I took creative writing and cultural studies classes.

As I mentally prepared to face what was waiting for me at home, I felt like a failure. I held the report card in my hand, got off the bus, and waited at home for my mother. I was sitting at the kitchen table doing homework when my mother walked in. I left my report card out in clear view and she instantly walked over to the table and picked it up. I looked up at her and took in the scowl I knew would be there.

"What is this?" She asked.

I remained silent.

"A *B*? And in math to boot." She continued.

"Momma, I –" I started.

"'Momma I.'" She said, mocking my attempt to explain. "Momma I nothing." Emphasizing the nothing, she slammed the report card on the table before speaking again. "Here I am teaching math to children every day and my child ain't got sense enough to get some help from her math teacher momma. I don't know how you plan on being a doctor making *B*'s."

I felt the back of my eyes heat up with shame and immediately sucked back the tears. Crying would only make things worse.

"So, what do you have to say for yourself?" She asked as she towered next to me. I stared at my open books, not wanting to look in her direction.

"I will do better next time." I said quickly, my eyes glued to the open pages in my book. I hoped those were the magic words to end our interaction.

"You better. I will not tolerate this type of nonsense in my house." She said and walked out of the kitchen. My eyes were blurred with tears and as I continued my homework, I did not dare let one fall.

After my tenth-grade hiccup, I regained footing and resumed my streak of *A*'s. While my mother's words still hurt, they no longer induced fear and her verbal vitriol no longer fueled my pursuits. I had come to expect scholastic perfection from myself. Becoming a doctor was no longer a childhood dream, it had become my plan for escape. I hoped that becoming a Millennium Scholar would be my way to finance everything. In a few short months, I would know if my prayers had been answered.

High school graduation day came and went with little fanfare, but the lack of recognition was not enough to take away my joy. I was elated. In the fall, I was moving to New Orleans. The recipients of the Millennium Scholarship would be announced in four weeks and I was riddled with anxiety. Justin suggested I visit him while he was staying with his mom in San Antonio, and I hoped the trip would help me with the wait. The seven days in Texas proved to add additional stressors as Justin's mom thought I was more of a "sidekick" than "wife material". I wore out my welcome when I told her my goals were bigger than being somebody's wife. I was supposed to ride back to Memphis with Justin and his dad in the next few days, but my mother and her boyfriend, Mr. Sims, drove down to pick me up. I butted in during my mother's tirade about my behavior.

"Have you received any news about the scholarship?" I asked eagerly.

"No, Rosalyn. I would have told you if I did. Stop asking. The news will come when it comes." My mother responded.

I spent the rest of the ride home in quiet anticipation.

The door to my room was closed as I approached. My heart sank as I reached for the knob. As the door swung open, my growing sense of anticipation climaxed into a high pitched shriek when I saw the large white envelope with Millennium in big bold print laying unopened on my bed.

"Momma!" I cried rushing to open the envelope."I thought you said nothing came!" I continued screaming. She came into the room, a look of confusion and worry on her face.

"Just open it, Rosalyn!"

With shaky hands I ripped open the envelope and pulled out

its contents. Reading the letter as fast as my eyes could scan the words, I leapt with joy when I read the correspondence.

Rosalyn Porter,

Congratulations! You have been selected to become a member of the inaugural class of The Bill and Melinda Gate's Millennium Scholars Program.

For a moment, all my prayers were answered. For a moment I was free from financial worry. For a moment, I was free to live away from my tyrant of a mother without feeling indebted to her; without needing her. My moment of joy was short lived. I howled like a wounded animal when I read there was a deadline for acceptance. That deadline was yesterday. Every piece of me to the tiniest particle shattered and I wailed with despair.

"Why didn't you know? Who checked the mailbox?" I screamed in a voice so full of hurt it did not sound like my own. My mother summoned the sibling and inquired about the letter. The sibling admitted to the act saying, "It had her name on it."

This was my ticket out and I would have been free, but the sibling checked the mail, put the letter on my bed, and closed my door. The sibling had heard me talk about my plan again and again. Enraged by the act of sabotage, I lashed out at the sibling.

"You knew I was not at home! What have you done? What have you done?" I screamed over and over with tears of fury clouding my vision.

The sibling responded, "If you weren't in Texas, you could have gotten your own mail."

I screamed and lunged at the sibling. As was customary, my mother quickly came to the sibling's defense. She said she would call in the morning and talk to someone. My mother tried to reassure me by offering a reminder that I was a scholarship recipient, and by suggesting that maybe something could be done. In a tear streaked daze, I stared through her finding irony in her statements.

I did not expect leniency from my own mother, so the thought of an organization granting me grace for missing a deadline was outside the realm of possibilities. After the futile phone call in which we learned that the scholarship was given to an alternate recipient, I retreated to my safe space. My cats cuddled next to me purring softly as I screamed into my pillow.

23

DON'T BE PATHETIC

I was devastated following the loss of the Millennium Scholarship and though I tried to mask my emotions, the cracks in my nonchalant façade deepened exposing the anger and sadness underneath. At the end of each day, I released my emotions in quiet fits of tears before falling asleep. One night as I sobbed deeply, the door to my room swung open.

"Rosalyn! You in here sleep?" My name sounded abrasive as it escaped my mother's lips. I quickly wiped my face and sat up in bed attempting to appear composed. I squinted as she flipped on the light and a tear rolled down my cheek. I knew she would notice.

"Where's your –?" She stopped and studied my face.

Here we go. I thought to myself.

"Are you in here crying?" She asked as she took a few steps into my room.

She glared at me and her hands moved from her sides to her hips.

Before I spoke, I urged myself to mask the sadness in my voice.

"Where's my what, Momma?" I countered feigning curiosity in her original inquiry. I avoided her second question altogether.

"What are you in here crying about?" She asked, the agitation in her voice becoming more apparent with each word.

"Nothing Momma. What were you looking for?" I asked again, hoping to successfully change the subject.

"Hell, I have forgotten now." She said staring at me menacingly as I returned her gaze from my bed.

"So, what are you crying about? Are you pregnant?" She yelled.

"No Momma! I am not pregnant!" I shouted back. I did not want this conversation to continue. Mere days had passed since I lost the scholarship. I did not think feeling bad about it merited an explanation.

My mother started to ask again but I stopped her.

"I am pissed off about losing that scholarship! It would have paid for *everything* all the way through medical school graduation! The way it happened was so messed up! I missed out on a life changing opportunity!"

The tears started making their way to my eyes. I breathed in deeply trying desperately to shove them back into the crevices from which they came, but it was no use. I had spoken my truth and hearing myself state my grievances out loud shattered my façade and the tears came tumbling down my face. My mother stood in my room, her hands still on her hips and studied my emotional meltdown with a critical squint.

"What's crying going to do?" She asked snidely. She turned to leave my room, but before exiting she added, "Stop being so pathetic." With those words, she turned and left my room slamming the door behind her.

I sniffled as I got out of bed and turned out the light. Laying back down, I was relieved to be alone. My mother had never been one to comfort me when I cried. As a young child she would snatch me up and say, "Stop all that crying before I give you something to cry about." The threat of corporal punishment prompted me to internalize my sobs.

In my teen years, my mother's tactics changed from physical to verbal. She had called me pathetic on countless occasions. My teenage desire to socialize brought about the first instance. It was common knowledge amongst my closest friends that extracurricular socialization was not allowed at my house, and I had cried after she refused to allow me to go out with my friends. The tears of anger mixed with the words "You don't ever let me do anything!" was met with "You don't need to do nothing. Stop all that fucking crying and acting so pathetic." Her words shocked me into silence.

The second time I was called pathetic was after a night with Joy at Appletree. It was my mother's turn to pick us up and drive Joy home. Joy and I giggled in the backseat when I used a swear word in a joke. The car came to a red light and my mom turned around and slapped me across the face.

"You ain't grown. Don't use that language around me. I'm still your mother!" She yelled. Her voice seemed too loud for the small car. I was embarrassed, and as I picked my glasses up from the floor of the back seat, I could feel the tears well up in my eyes. My mother looked at me warningly and I turned to the window avoiding her gaze. Joy and I "stopped all the noise" and the rest of the car ride to Joy's home was silent. After saying goodbye to Joy, I kept my head down in the car. The sting of tears in my eyes threatened to fall down my face with every bump in the road.

As soon as we got home, I ran to my room. My mother seemed to follow me, taunting me, ready to pounce with the first tear that fell. I had not yet escaped her line of sight when the tears silently made their way down my cheeks. It seemed to give her joy to call me pathetic. This time her words not only shocked me, but the intent seemed malicious and that hurt like hell.

Pathetic became my mother's go to within her already colorful arsenal of insults for all occasions in which I displayed the tiniest inkling of vulnerability. Crying for any reason was deemed unacceptable. Once after an argument with Justin, she barged into my room as I was hanging up from the emotional call.

"I know you not in here crying over some boy." She said scowling. I looked up at her with anger in my eyes as she looked down on me with disgust. "Don't be pathetic." She said and rolled her eyes.

The shock of it eventually wore away, but each time my mother called me pathetic it hurt. Unwilling to taint sacred time with friends with my ongoing mother drama, I dealt with the emotional wounds internally. On the occasions where I could feel the bite coming, I would attempt to detach myself from the situation. Just as I hovered above myself as a ten-year-old child while RP robotically interacted with the Retops, I would watch my interactions with my mother in third person. I would give her small responses, just so she could not accuse me of not listening. With RP in the driver's seat, I was prepared for her verbally abusive onslaughts. When she finally pounced, my emotions were guarded by my unflappable alter ego.

I also dealt with the pain and hurt creatively. I wrote poems and wrote stories fantasizing about a life of freedom and adventure. The characters in my stories had unbridled love affairs with life, and I longed for my life's tale to take me to a land far, far away.

Mostly, I dealt with the hurt through rationalization. If I could create an understanding surrounding an event, no matter the merits of my assumptions, my pain would dissipate. This was the approach I took with the verbal offenses. The word pathetic angered me immensely. It bothered me that one word could cause me to come unglued. It was the way she said it. My mother emphasized the word and used it pointedly, as if her words were not simply insulting but based in fact. I knew what pathetic meant, but I needed to dissect the word. I needed to understand how she could say that to me, her daughter.

Clearly, she did not mean I was miserably inadequate. I was an honor student, first chair saxophonist, an All-West blue-ribbon recipient several years running, I had been an athlete, had several jobs, and would be able to attend any college I chose.

The other definition of pathetic, arousing pity through sadness, caught my attention. Each time she used the word, I had been crying or in an otherwise vulnerable state. I was disgusted by the thought that I would cry to get anyone to coddle me, especially her. She had never been overindulgent in caring about me or any of my interests. She had never come to a track meet, band performance, or induction ceremony. I tried hard to be a perfect student and besides by blistering temper, I kept my nose clean. Despite my efforts, I had been left to fend for myself in every situation that would have garnered parental support. If being the best at just about everything did not earn me a place in her good graces, crying, an act I knew she despised, would not help if gaining her favor were my agenda. I found it asinine that I would cry to gain favor or pity from anyone.

The thought of being vulnerable around others and having them pity me, repulsed me after that. I learned to respond to emotionally charged events with intellectual coolness and emotional distance. Rationalization became my weapon of choice and crying in front of people became a thing of the past. I did not trust anyone with my tears, and I did not desire pity. I journaled and found comfort in working through my sadness. I resolved any state of discontent with written question and answer sessions and sought a deeper understanding of my disposition. I needed to have control over my emotions. By choosing to analyze the things that bothered me, the pain started to vanish. Soon, my mother's words no longer induced shock and hurt and I became apathetic to her insults.

While my outward disposition was even, my insides became at odds with themselves during fits of rage or intense sadness. Situations that would have normally evoked tears now created a churning in the pit of my stomach. Most times this was easy enough to hide, however on occasion the somatic reaction was so violent it stopped me in my tracks causing me to then rush to the bathroom. I would soon learn to control that response as well.

As the years went by, sympathy and pity became equivalents. Stoic and detached, I did not discuss the turmoil of my home life with my friends. Distanced from the topics that concerned most of my teen peers and with my emotions tucked away, I became the go-to person for unfiltered and rational advice. I was thoughtful, objective, and direct. My friends would say, "Rosalyn doesn't sugarcoat shit". I found it easy to come up with quick solutions to their life crises and found their sense of urgency unnecessary. I envied the emotional bandwidth that they could give to dating and spats with peers. The nature of their concerns paled in comparison to my daily struggle for peace and sanity.

The night after losing the scholarship I slipped. The mask of nonchalance had cracked, and I was unable to suppress my emotions. My self-soothing session had been interrupted and I was caught with my emotional pants down. As I lay in bed piecing together a new escape plan, I vowed to never let my mother see me vulnerable again. I upgraded my armor, and that night was the last time I cried in front of my mother. She would never have another opportunity to call me pathetic.

24

LOST FAITH

"*The Lord is Here. The Lord is Here. The Lord. The Lord. Is here.*" The congregation stood as the Alpha Church choir sang *The Lord is Here*. The choir marched into the church slowly, their footsteps matching the lyrics' adagio tempo. Their white and black bottomed choir gowns swayed against the burgundy carpeted aisles as they continued their march into the choir stand. The clergy members, distinguished in all white, repeated the slow methodic entrance to the altar as the choir continued their hymn. *"The Lord is here. The Lord is here. The Lord. The Lord. Is here."*

Standing in the choir side pews, I shifted uncomfortably in my heels and sighed. I fought my facial expressions and the urge to tap impatiently on the wooden pew in front of me. The choir continued. *"He is here. He is here. The Lord is here."* The Alpha Church service had been the same since I was a little girl. Sometimes I could still hear my father's booming and passionate voice from the pulpit. Even when the choir sang, his voice rang out distinctly from the rest. With the thought of my father, a lump caught in my throat. I lowered my head and closed my eyes. After the opening prayer, the congregation sat, and Sunday service was officially underway.

Dragged to church Sunday after Sunday, I sat in the same pews usually sandwiched between the sibling and some person unknown. The preacher's interminable sermon would drag on oftentimes lulling me to sleep only to be startled awake by a pinch from my mother. The preacher would eventually end with "Can I get an Amen?". The congregation always answered the preacher's call with shouts of "Amen!" Staccato chords and melodic flourishes from the organist emphasized the call and response until the Holy Spirit compelled a member of the congregation to stand to their feet and dance in the aisles. The swell of energy would erupt through the church and soon several members were up on their feet clapping, dancing, and shouting. I would watch the people overtaken by this unseen Holy Ghost and wondered if it were real or a performance.

This Sunday's church service would look just the same as the others, but it was different. It was the last Sunday I would be forced to go "praise the Lord". While we went to church each Sunday, my family was not a religious one. There was no talk of God at home or any mandatory recitation of Grace before dinner nor prayers at bedtime. As a child, I only prayed for one person. Each night, I closed my eyes and prayed that my daddy would have good health and a long life. The night he was carried out on the stretcher, I prayed hard that he would come back. I prayed so hard that I felt like I would break. My only prayers would go unanswered. After that going to church was just another chore.

My mother advised me to "pray about it" after losing the Bill and Melinda Gates Millennium Scholarship. I was infuriated by the trite words and quick dismissal of my monumental loss. What had transpired had nothing to do with prayer, and prayer was not going to get my scholarship back. Weeks later, I received notification that based upon my GPA, I was awarded an academic scholarship from Xavier University. The scholarship covered tuition and on-site housing. It was not the Millennium scholarship, but I was grateful. Books and living expenses would be up to me, which meant getting a job. I would have to focus on paying for medical school later. When I informed my mother about my scholarship from Xavier, she ranted about how I needed to thank God for my blessing. I gave her a stone-faced look and returned to my room. I worked hard in school to get the GPA that afforded me that scholarship while enduring living in *this* house. I did not understand what God had to do with it.

"Let us worship and bow down. Let us kneel before the Lord." I read the words written on the Alpha Church altar as Bishop William L. Jones made his way to the microphone.

"We are going to talk about *faith* today church." He started speaking. His voice was full and commanded attention. He emphasized the word faith saying it loudly into the microphone. The word echoed against the stained glass adorned walls. Bishop Jones glanced at his notes before starting again.

"*Faith* is an unshakeable belief in something without proof or evidence." He closed his notes.

"Walk with me church." Bishop Jones said.

A member shouted, "All right now!"

The Bishop continued. "Now the word says 'Yea, though I walk through the valley of the shadow of death, I will fear no evil: for thou art with me; thy rod and thy staff they comfort me.' You must have *FAITH*!"

"Amen!" The congregation shouted.

As the preacher dissected his message on faith in God, I watched as those around me nodded and vocalized in agreement. My mother nodded along as well, and I again fought the urge to roll my eyes. I found the ferocious tiger mom nodding at teachings of good faith works and kindness hypocritical. I had come to believe a lot of folks "following the word of God" were performing. Even Justin's mom taught Bible study the week I visited yet cursed and exiled me from her home.

I sat in silence half listening to the sermon and wondered how one could have faith in some unseen entity. I believed in science, objective data, and reasoning. I believed in observation and the identification of patterns. I believed in evolution and the big bang. I wrote a paper once using an assignment to try and fuse religion with evolution. I suggested that days in the Bible were not twenty-four-hour time periods as we know them and were possibly the billions of years coinciding with the evolutionary timeline. I received an *A* on the paper; however, it did not satisfy my doubts in the teachings on Sundays.

Religion was like a fairytale. One where putting trust in an omnipotent omnipresent being would grant you blessings and abundance. One where those ordained by God could lay hands on a person and they were healed. One where people could act in the most atrocious ways, ask for forgiveness, and the stench of sin was washed away. As I scanned the members of the congregation, each person listening intently to the Bishop's words, I thought to myself, maybe some people needed to believe in fairytales. Maybe there were those who needed to put their faith in something outside of themselves to find peace, motivation, or hope. I was not one of those people, and it had been a long time since I believed in fairytales.

At the climax of the preacher's sermon, the organist's musical stylings sent the church into an uproar. The choir started singing, and soon many in the congregation were up on their feet. The usual parties caught the Holy Spirit and a few jostled around with seizure like motions. After the conclusion of the sermon, the choir sang *While I'm Down Here Praying, Lord Search My Heart*, and Bishop Jones invited the congregation to the altar. The congregation stood, and in an orderly fashion walked through the aisles taking turns kneeling at the altar.

The choir continued, *"While I'm down here praying, Lord search my heart. Search my heart, search my heart, search my heart."* I knelt slowly at the altar and lowered my head. If the Lord were indeed searching my heart, He would find a proud young woman. A young woman that despite challenging circumstances was living up to her father's words and who had survived her mother's abuse. He would find a fighter devoid of faith in anything and anyone outside of herself. He would find a young woman whose faith lay in her abilities, ambitions, and her determination to live a life of her own design. The choir continued *"Search my heart, search my heart, search my heart."* I lifted my head, rose to my feet, and returned to my seat.

The morning had rolled into afternoon and the service was coming to an end. During the closing announcements, my mother stood. I looked to her with curiosity in my eyes. She announced that I would be attending Xavier University of Louisiana on an academic scholarship and would be leaving for New Orleans this week. Her announcement was met with some applause and a chorus of "Praise God" from various members of the congregation. My mother ended her announcement by thanking people in advance for their prayers. As the members filed out of church, several approached me and congratulated me on my endeavors. They wished me well, and they all said they would be "praying for me". I wanted to say, "Thanks but no thanks". I did not trust anyone to pray for me as I only counted on myself to have my best interests at heart. I was my own savior. I smiled politely, shook hands, and thanked them for their well wishes. Then I said goodbye to Alpha Church.

I spent most of my last week in Memphis with Justin. He had returned from San Antonio in preparation to matriculate to West Point to attend the US Military Academy Preparatory School. Despite being a stellar student-athlete and heavily recruited by top SEC schools, his mother convinced him that USMAPS would be in his best interest. Although Justin wanted to go to a big football school to pursue his dream of playing in the NFL, he succumbed to his mother's reasoning and decided on USMAPS. I did not understand his choice and I told him, "If football is your dream, you should go to where you can make the most of that opportunity. I understand getting an education as well, but you can get a great education anywhere if you apply yourself." He agreed with most of my words but graduating as an officer would make his mother proud, and that superseded his NFL hopes.

Despite Justin attending USMAPS and my going XULA, we decided to maintain our relationship. We bought a safe and filled it with movie ticket stubs, restaurant receipts, photo booth pictures, and prom invitations, all items from our romantic journey to date. We also added promises for the future. We promised to remain faithful to one another and to stay the same people the other fell in love with. While I loved Justin and was willing to try, I secretly envied his faith in us. Justin believed deeply in our love and held the unwavering view that our relationship was special. He knew we would do what everyone, including his mother doubted; make it.

My sister, Daphne, and my mother drove me to New Orleans early that Saturday morning. After dropping off the last box in my new home in St. Joe's Hall, I excitedly said goodbye to my family. The sense of relief that washed over me as I returned to my room to unpack was overwhelming. I cried unbridled happy tears as I continued to unpack. As the tears flowed, the weight of my childhood and adolescence was lifted and I was ready to live my life as an independent adult whose faith lay only in her works.

My first semester at XULA seemed to pass too quickly, and before I knew it, I was back in Memphis for Christmas break. I had mixed emotions about coming home. While I was excited to see Justin, I was not thrilled about being back under my mother's roof, even in a temporary capacity. I got a holiday job at The Ham Company and spent the remainder of my free time with Justin. So far, he and I had done well maintaining our long-distance relationship and all signs pointed to continued success.

It was my idea to watch *The Family Man*. It looked like a fun holiday film, and as a Nicolas Cage fan, I was excited to see it.

Justin and I cozied up on the couch and started the film. The movie introduced us to college sweethearts Jack and Kate. Jack is about to embark on a yearlong internship of his dreams with the Barclays in London. As Jack prepares to board his flight, Kate expresses her fears that their relationship will not survive the distance and pleads with Jack not to leave. Jack attempts to reassure Kate saying their relationship is strong enough to last and leaves to pursue his career opportunity. The audience later learns that the relationship did not survive and reintroduces us to Jack thirteen years later, successful and wealthy, but his life is one without Kate.

"Would you have gotten on the plane?" Justin asked.

"Yeah, I'm with Jack on this one." I responded. I quickly noticed the change in Justin's demeanor.

"Would you have gotten on the plane?" I asked.

"No. If you thought my leaving would be detrimental to our relationship, I would stay with you." He said firmly.

"So you're telling me that if it came between our relationship and pursuing your dream of going to the NFL—" I started. Justin answered the question before I could finish.

"I would choose us." He stated and with a pained expression he asked, "You wouldn't?"

I considered his words and asked for clarification. "If it came between us and choosing to be a doctor?" "Yeah, exactly." He replied.

I paused. I knew what I was supposed to say. I knew Justin was looking for me to reassure him. He was looking for me to demonstrate that same unshakeable belief in our relationship that he had.

"I have wanted to be a doctor my whole life. By comparison, our relationship is a drop in the bucket." I said shrugging. My words silenced him. I stopped the DVD and turned to him. We sat in silence and I watched as the hurt spread across his face.

"I am sure we will have to make decisions like that somewhere along the line. What's the point of our relationship if I can't count on you to choose me?" He asked with cracks in his voice and pleading eyes. I searched my heart for an alleviation to his pain and for the faith that he needed from me.

    I was nineteen years old and had been in three weddings. A flower girl in the first, a junior bridesmaid in the second, and a bridesmaid in the third. In all three ornate celebrations of love, I watched as the bride and groom pronounced their eternal love for one another before God and an audience of friends and family. They all ended with the happy couples riding off into the sunset to a chorus of cheers and cascades of confetti. After each wedding, the dresses I wore went into a trunk. The white flower girl dress I wore in my oldest sister's wedding was still perfect with its scooped neckline, thin black satin belt, and black ribboned hem line. The champagne laced simple gown and the rich royal blue junior bridesmaid dress were untouched and just as beautiful as the day I wore them. Unlike the never changing dresses, each of the happy couples dissolved into distant duos destined for divorce. Happily, ever after was another fairytale that I did not believe in. Justin was right, I could not guarantee that I would choose him. With tears in my eyes, I responded.

    "I would not want you to give up your dreams for me, just as I will not give up my dreams for you." It was my final answer and with those words I had shattered Justin's faith, and our relationship was over.

THIRD PARTY PERCEPTIONS

I returned to Xavier, and while I had lost a great friend, the breakup with Justin meant one less thing distracting me from my new goal, a scholarship to medical school. I went to class in sweats or jeans, hoodies, and sneakers. My hair, always curly in the humidity of New Orleans was usually in a high messy bun. Positioning myself with a bird's eye view, I would sit in a back corner of the classroom and watch as my classmates engaged around me. Picking up on several conversations at once, I would tune in and out as if flipping stations, disinterested in one channel after the next. If someone started a conversation, I would chat for a bit, however if there was not a natural curiosity, I simply lost interest, fell silent and waited for class to start. Laser focused; I dove headfirst into the challenging course load. Xavier, a liberal arts college, not only excelled in preparing students for medical school, but also ensured that we had a well rounded education. In addition to my core pre-medical curriculum, I took theology, philosophy, and creative writing. I enjoyed picking apart information and developing a deeper understanding and appreciation for the various subjects. School had always been the easy part but the education I would receive while attending Xavier University extended beyond the classroom.

Finally distanced from the social limitations placed upon me by my mother, I explored my environment and hopped in and out of social circles. Even outside of my restrictive home, I learned that I preferred cats and my own company to that of others. I found myself triggered by everyday gossip and the playful name calling amongst peers. My temper was incited even further when these initially innocuous jests escalated into explosive emotional exchanges. Reminded of the home I had escaped; I would feel the swell of anger rise in my chest. When my temper reached its limits, I would retreat to the solitude of my room. I was self-aware enough to know that if any of the derogatory *jokes* were hurled in my direction, I would be the one to swing first. Safeguarding myself and others, I was again a cat in a box, happily isolated from my peers. I developed a few close friendships, otherwise I was selectively social and did not involve myself in the day-to-day drama of college life. I was at Xavier University for a reason, and I did not need any distractions from my goal.

Selective socialization and hard work were paying off until my original roommate decided to leave school and I was paired with someone new. Shannon was from Shreveport Louisiana and we were complete opposites. She was messy, loud, and there was nothing selective about when or how she socialized. People would drop by our room no matter the day or time. When I addressed my concerns directly, Shannon would cry and tell me that "I hurt her feelings". When she and her guests would have raucous conversations as I sat studying at my desk, I tried an indirect approach. If they got too loud, I would turn to her and give her a look that suggested her disregard for my studying was disrespectful. Catching my drift, Shannon would giggle and apologize. Sometimes, she and her posse would change venues for their gathering.

Shannon also snored. Ever since my childhood night terrors, I had become a light sleeper and had bouts with insomnia. I would lay in bed staring at Shannon's bunk above me hoping for a break in the cacophony of her guttural rattling. After several weeks of disruptive visitors and sleepless nights, we had a conversation and set some boundaries, however our talk did little to improve our discordant relationship. I was direct, honest, and even-keeled, during my talks with Shannon, yet she perceived me as "mean" and "crazy". Unbothered by her perception, I bought earplugs and longed for the times she was away visiting nearby family. It was the only time there was peace and quiet and I was granted the serenity to focus on my goal. I was determined to get a scholarship to medical school.

It was a challenging semester, I was taking eighteen credit hours and working part time at Weiner's, a department store blocks away from campus. My course load included organic chemistry and to this point was the most challenging class of my educational career. I sat at my desk, threw my head back, closed my eyes, and sighed as I leaned back in my chair balancing the seat on its hind legs. I had been studying all morning and was tired after another night of disjointed sleep. I placed my chair back on all fours and checked the time. I had work in a few hours. I closed my notes on stereochemistry and arose from my desk. I lay atop the lavender comforter and covered my legs with the quilted throw. I closed my eyes and napped. The alarm on my twenty-five-disc CD changer sitting on the shelf next to my desk seemed to go off almost instantly. I groggily got up, showered, and got ready for work. Before leaving the room, I made my bed, tidied my desk, and prepared for classes the next day.

I was exhausted upon my return from Weiner's. I walked sleepily through the lobby and waved at a few classmates who noticed my entrance. It was movie night, and the lobby was filled with coeds. I hoped Shannon was among them. Continuing to the elevator, I rested my head on the silver metallic surface as it ascended to the fourth floor. The closer I got to my room, the heavier my footsteps were. I felt as though I was pulling my body inch by inch through an invisible force field that pushed back against my every step. Finally, with my room in sight and visions of sleeping dancing in my head, exhaustion was replaced by irritation as I stood at the door. Loud music and laughter were coming from the room. Fuck! I thought to myself and sighed deeply.

"Get a grip RP." I said aloud as I took another deep breath and turned the key.

I opened the door and my eyes darted around the room. The blaring bass filled music muted the sound of my entrance and I went unnoticed as I stood in the room's entryway. Taking in detail after detail, I became less exhausted and the grip on my temper loosened. The music was coming from my stereo and the small television on my desk was on. Shannon and friends were laughing and frolicking and to add insult to injury, someone was even sitting on my bed. I forcefully entered the room and went directly to my desk and turned off my stereo. I glared at Shannon before turning to the stranger on my bed.

"Get your ass off of my bed, now!" I said loudly and with unquestionable force. The girl sitting in the bottom bunk scurried away. I looked at Shannon. "So what? Just fuck me and my belongings, huh?" It was quiet in the room now, but my voice was just as filled with bass as the music.

"I-I-I'm sorry." Shannon stuttered.

"Yeah, you are sorry!" I snapped. "We had an entire house rules conversation and I explicitly stated don't touch my things without my permission."

Shannon's friend attempted to intervene on her behalf.

I whipped my head around toward the speaking party. The girl who was sitting on my bed did not have an opportunity to finish her statement.

"Fuck what you are talking about. You're the idiot who had your big disrespectful ass all up in my bed. Bitch I sleep there! As a matter of fact, all of y'all get the fuck out before I throw somebody out the window!"

A small audience had gathered in the hall in front of our room. Shannon's eyes started to water, and she burst into tears. I stood glaring and my chest heaved, as Shannon and her friends left the room and closed the door. I got out of my work clothes, lay in bed, and closed my eyes. Shannon did not return to our room that night, and I was finally able to sleep.

After acing my organic chemistry test, I bopped happily down the street toward the LLC. I entered the dorm and was met by stares from many of the students occupying the residence hall lobby. I gave an aloof little wave and continued towards my room. Before I could press the elevator call button, I was approached by the residence hall director.

"Rosalyn Porter?"

I turned to face the inquiring party.

"That is correct." I answered.

"I am Stacy Frank the residence hall director. Do you have time to talk?"

"Sure." I responded.

I followed the woman to a small office space and took a seat in a chair at a circular table.

"I want to talk to you about the incident that took place between you and Shannon last night."

A straight-faced expression was my only response. After a brief pause, Miss Frank continued.

"Shannon and her friends stated there was a verbal altercation and you threatened to throw them out of a window. Is this true?"
"That is correct." I said looking at her, blinking slowly.

The residence hall director's lashes fluttered quickly as if surprised by my response. She studied my facial expression and body language.

"Do you agree that it would be more peaceful not to threaten our roommates?" She asked. It was a loaded question, so I asked one of my own.

"Peaceful to whom?"

Miss Frank again looked as if my response did not compute. She paused before restarting.

"So, am I to gather that you are not remorseful about your words or actions?" She asked.

"That is correct." I answered.

"Why is that?" She asked.

"Thank you for finally asking for anything from my perspective." I said sarcastically. "Shannon and her friends were disrespecting my space and tampering with my personal property. This is not the first time that Shannon and I have spoken about her lack of consideration and common courtesy. In my opinion, she brought this on herself."

Miss Frank looked at me wide-eyed. I could tell that if this was a test, I had failed. Miss Frank thanked me for my time, and I was dismissed.

Shannon moved out later that week. She felt unsafe, and our altercation activated her anxiety. Informed of the details in a letter, I was relieved to learn that I would not have another roommate for the remainder of the semester. I also learned that I was no longer an appropriate candidate for on campus housing and that this semester would be my last at the Living and Learning Center dorm.

The news spread quickly, and the residence hall was filled with murmurs about Rosalyn, "the crazy, mean girl." The girl getting "kicked out" because I "beat up" my roommate. I discovered Shannon had a flair for storytelling, and the verbal assault was edited to also include a physical one. The rumor spread, and although it was full of half-truths, I did not attempt to correct third-party perceptions. I was quick tempered and slow to warm up to others. I was strong-willed and outspoken. I knew exactly who I was and did not feel obligated to share that person with anyone. I chose when and who I interacted with based on a self-created code. A code where respect was paramount, and drama was not tolerated. If the consensus was that I was mean and crazy, so be it; I had been called worse.

Unfazed, I continued to work, go to class, and study. When the mood struck, I would accompany the few friends I had to parties or campus events. At those times I traded my hoodie, jeans, and sneakers for more form fitting attire and heels. Relaxed, jubilant, and charismatic, my personality accented with coiffed hair and lipstick, I was unrecognizable to my peers. Oftentimes, people would tell stories about "crazy Rosalyn" with me sitting nearby. My adolescence had left me with thick skin, and instead of hurting or taking offense I was entertained by the perpetuated slander. My classmates' behaviors were expected. I had come to believe people enjoyed hurting others and fed off drama. I would listen until they got to an integral part of the story, then pop over and introduce myself with a glare and a smile. Their jaws dropping to the floor made for fun stories of my own to share once I returned to my friends.

After moving into an off-campus apartment with my best friend, I spent even less time on campus. Losing the housing stipend meant longer hours at work, but it was still not enough. Eventually, I folded and asked my mother for help. Every time she wrote me a check, I was haunted by the loss of the Millennium Scholarship which drove me to work even harder. I had to get a scholarship for medical school. That was my one and only goal and I used Xavier University as a tool.

School and socialization were kept separate. I partied in the city of New Orleans into the wee hours of the morning with only the company of my roommate and a few other close friends. Returning to campus, my demeanor was one of quiet focus. Being perceived as mean and crazy was water off a duck back.

Two months into my senior year at XULA, I received my acceptance letter to Vanderbilt University School of Medicine. I would smile inwardly with pride as I walked past my name and photo in the "Accepted!" display case that occupied the front hall of the Arts and Sciences Center. The looks of awe and disbelief I received from my peers made the accomplishment even sweeter. Weeks later, I would receive the icing on the cake. I had been awarded a scholarship to medical school.

26

REFUGE

"Rosalyn Porter, Magna Cum Laude."

The announcer's deep voiced bellowed through the auditorium as I walked across the stage with my head high. I smiled broadly, beaming with pride when the Dean of the College of Arts and Sciences handed me my college diploma. I took the diploma with one hand and shook the Dean's hand with the other. I could hear Joy and my sisters cheering from the bleachers as I continued my walk across the graduation stage. I shot my best friend and roommate a thumbs up and a wink when I made it back to my seat.

"Congratulations Xavier University class of 2003!"

Cheers and applause filled the auditorium, and we tossed our caps into the air.

"Rosalyn!" Joy's voice screeched in my ear as she hugged me warmly.

"I am so happy you could make it!" I shouted gleefully.

"I wouldn't miss it! Let me see!" Joy said excitedly while reaching for my diploma. I opened my diploma and posed with my hand on my hip and a smile. Joy laughed and continued jokingly, "Dang girl! Look at these stripes! Did you get *all* the honors?"

I laughed and looked down at the yellow, red, and white honor cords and the gold honors sash around my neck.

"Thanks Joy!" I giggled.

Joy told me she knew where my family was, and we talked animatedly as we made our way outside. I spotted them in the sea of black graduation gowns standing alongside the auditorium's outer walls. Still smiling as I approached, my sisters greeted me with "Congratulations Rosalyn!" I hugged my nieces, nephews, and sisters, and thanked them for their words. While in an embrace with my oldest sister, I caught a glimpse of my mother from the corner of my eye. Dressed in a white pants suit with a black scooped neck shirt underneath and a black and white bow around her neck, she glared at the celebratory scene before her. Her eyes were squinted and low and her jaw was clenched. I closed my eyes and took a deep breath before releasing my sister from our embrace.

"Let's take some photos!" Joy's cheerful voice diverted my attention back to the happy occasion.

I posed with my family, standing tall and brimming with accomplishment.

"Smile Mrs. Porter! It's a graduation!" Joy said with laughter in her voice.

I did not look to see if my mother had taken Joy's advice. I was not going to let her bother me today. Today I was on cloud nine.

My roommate and my boyfriend came over to greet my family. I introduced my beau to my sisters. Looking towards my mother, I said "Mom, this is Trent." She looked in our direction, rolled her eyes, and walked away. I shook my head and went back to my friends.

"Is she ok?" Trent asked.

"I'm not sure." I paused. "She always treats me like that." I said with a shrug. I could feel the sting trying to make an appearance in my chest and behind my eyes. Not today. I thought forcefully. Today will not be about her. You made it, and her approval is not required. Its onward and upward from here. With that internal pep talk, I swallowed down the emotion and celebrated my academic milestone with friends and the city of New Orleans. I promised myself that night to never let anyone steal my joy.

Graduation from medical school was like Groundhog's Day. I was gowned and draped, surrounded by friends and family, with a smile so big it made my head hurt, yet my mother looked unimpressed, as if the fanfare for my achievements were trifles and she would rather be at home in bed.

Learning I had matched at my number one residency program in Chicago sent me over the moon and I could not be happier to be so far away from home. During the time in residency, I was too busy for preoccupation with family and used the excuse of the workload to avoid returning home. When the University of Chicago Obstetrics and Gynecology residency class of 2011 celebrated the end of a long journey, my mother rolled her eyes while I gave my graduation speech. She was outwardly hostile with the residency program director and did not utter a word as Dr. Blane introduced herself and gushed about me.

After residency, fellow rising physicians looked for jobs in hometowns or places near family or friends. My best friends were scattered around the country and I was not tethered to family. For me, even the thought of being closer to home was enough to cloud my disposition, so I decided to stay in Chicago. I had just turned thirty years old and after twelve years of post-high school education and training, the only desire I had was to finally live.

Passion propelled my pursuits, and I secured a position with an organization providing care to underserved communities. It was fulfilling to finally start my career and I felt accomplished and proud of my work. The actualization of becoming the woman I strived to be, was intoxicating. I had stared in the face of death and maneuvered through childhood depression. I had absorbed emotional abuse and used it to create fuel for focus. I had channeled my teen rage into empowerment and had triumphed over the rigors of medical education and training. I had removed myself from toxic relationships and fortified my independence. I was ready to enjoy the fruits of my labor. With work hard play harder as my motto, I decided to move to Chicago's West Loop neighborhood to be closer to the action. The moment I stepped into the twenty first floor two-bedroom, two full bathroom corner unit in the Park Alexandria, I had to have it. My eyes widened as I looked out at the city from the floor to ceiling windows that wrapped around the west and north walls. Both bedrooms were spacious, but the owner's suite had a beautiful, marbled bathroom with a large, jetted tub as well as a standalone rain shower. The condo was complete with a state-of-the-art kitchen and in house washer and dryer. The best part was the long wraparound balcony, which would prove perfect for morning coffee.

Operating from my new West Loop address, I cultivated a bachelorette lifestyle and reveled in life unscripted. I indulged in the various Chicago restaurants and bars and participated in the city's endless events. I went to music festivals, beer festivals, Pride festivals, and street festivals. I went to sporting events and concerts and frequented museums and art galleries. I went to house parties and block parties and danced the night away at clubs. Aside from enjoying Chicago, I traveled incessantly both domestic and abroad. Each day brought a new opportunity for an adventure and I took full advantage. Some days while enjoying the view from my West Loop condo, with Sox and Scrappy my only company, I would become overwhelmed with giddiness and burst into laughter. I could not remember ever being so happy.

I LEFT MY SOUTHSIDE OFFICE AND HOPPED IN MY GOLD HONDA Civic. It had been a long week, and I was thankful it was Friday. My phone rang, and for a second, I was distracted. The impact jerked me forward and then slammed my body back into the driver's seat. In a haze of confusion, I shook my head and tried to focus my senses. The phone that I had reached for was on the floor. I picked it up and tapped the screen for a response. As the phone's screen lit up in my hand, I noticed the people in the street. I could hear them asking if I was ok through the rolled-up windows. I could barely see out of the windshield; the hood of my car had been folded onto itself. I had not seen brake lights and was still confused when I hopped out of the car to assess the damage. The Civic that I had since college was totaled.

The police arrived on the scene and I waited in my car as they spoke to the other driver. In a turn of events, the person that I hit from behind had broken taillights and had a warrant out for their arrest. I was not given a ticket and was free to go. I made a few calls, had my car towed, and a friend took me home.

I filed a claim and received a quote for the totaled car from my insurance company. The company paid for a rental while I waited on the check. Reviewing the paperwork, I noticed that the check was to be received at my mother's Memphis address. Unable to change that on my end, I called my mother and filled her in on the event's that transpired.

After detailing the accident and discussing the insurance claim, I told my mother to look out for the check. I asked her to take my address so that she could send it to me when it arrived.

"Do you think I am just going to send that check to you?" She asked and the question was like a punch in the gut. I held the phone in my hands and shook my head. Not knowing what to say, I asked a question.

"What do you mean?"

"That is my car. I paid for it. So, if it is totaled and there is a check coming, that is my money." My mother stated definitively.

My heart sank. I asked another question.

"So what do you suggest I do for transportation?"

"You are a doctor now; you'll figure it out." She responded and hung up the phone.

I had only been an attending for a couple of months. I had no savings and no credit, but after Hawaii and now this, I refused to call her back and beg. I kept the rental for as long as possible while I saved money to purchase a car. Even worlds away, my mother found a way to slap me in the face.

Months later, I got a phone call about my maternal grandmother's passing and the impending funeral. My stomach twisted into knots in response to the news. I had mixed memories of my maternal grandmother. The good ones were, made from scratch biscuits before elementary school, holding hands on walks to and from school, and laughing and clapping at the television while watching game shows. The bad ones were whippings with switches and her fights with Mother. It had been years since I had seen my maternal grandmother, but I was expected to be at the funeral all the same.

My alarm went off at 5:00 a.m. on the day of the funeral. I reached for my phone and silenced the rapidly repeating beep. I sat at the edge of my bed in the dark and listened to the rain rapping rhythmically against the window. A slight sense of dread made itself noticeable in the pit of my stomach. I took a few deep breaths and groggily made my way to the bathroom. I felt more awake after my quick shower, but the water did little to alleviate the growing sensation in my gut. Ignoring the discomfort, I gathered my things and headed to the garage. My flight boarded in a little over two and a half hours and I wanted to give myself ample time given the rain. I put my overnight bag in the backseat and hopped in the car. The funeral was at 1:00 p.m. I would get to Memphis with enough time to change and get to the service. Afterwards, I would have a few moments with family and then fly back to Chicago.

The rain beat heavily against the windshield of my Toyota Camry. I flicked the wipers and turned them to the highest speed. The heavy rainfall made for low visibility and I pushed my hazard lights on as I turned onto the highway. "Ugh, my stomach hurts." I said aloud as I turned off the car radio. The beating rain, the sound of the wipers dragging across the windshield, and the flicking of the hazard lights provided enough of a soundtrack for the drive.

My stomach continued to churn, and the new car smell was sickening as I was overtaken by waves of nausea. I cracked my windows enough for fresh air, but not enough to allow the rain to drench the car's interior. I slowed my driving speed and gulped in the air, hoping it would alleviate the nausea.

When Chicago's O'Hare Airport came into view everything spiraled. My palms became sweaty. My pulse and breathing quickened. The waves of nausea were so violent that I pulled into a nearby parking lot, got out, and kneeled beside my car. Soon enough I was vomiting in the rain until there was nothing left. I sat in the car for a while with my head down and shaky hands resting on the steering wheel. I had just had a panic attack. I did not know whether the trigger was attending the funeral or being home, but what I did know was that I was not going anywhere. I left the lot and headed back towards my haven in the West Loop.

Shaken by my anxiety attack, I decided to incorporate more self-care into my routine. In addition to more physical activity and spa treatments, I got a therapist. A co-worker and friend gave me the contact information for Dr. Danielle K. Evans. I started seeing Dr. Evans regularly. I knew that my childhood and adolescence had left scars, but I needed to unpack the internal wounds. I associated going home with turmoil and discomfort. Although the interactions with my mother were hurtful, I discovered what hurt most was wanting things to be different. Over the course of my therapy, I let go of the anger and expectations. People were who they were including parents and that was ok. I also stopped feeling guilty about the disdain I had for her and about rejecting daughterly duties. I learned that it was also ok to distance myself and set healthy boundaries.

For the very first time, I had found peace and felt light as a feather. I continued to create the space I needed to live freely and to fall in love with the woman I had become. No longer seeking an escape, and no longer needing a refuge, I started to wonder if Chicago was my forever home.

27

EVERYTHING BUT DOMESTIC

As departmental business continued to dwindle in Chicago, administration days were spent in the comfort of my home. Sitting cross legged on the couch in my spotless living room with a freshly laundered throw covering my legs, I chewed on my pen top thinking about my life and staring out of the streak free floor to ceiling windows. Every so often I would jot down an idea on the notepad sitting in my lap. I absentmindedly absorbed the Chicago city skyline and the distant sound of trains passing on the tracks below.

Startled by a knock at my door, I hopped off the sofa and walked barefoot across the freshly waxed hardwood floors.

"The doorman did not call up." I said aloud and looked through the peephole. "Oh! I forgot you were coming!" I said as I turned the deadbolt lock and opened the door.

"Hey Rosalyn." Cheryl, my personal chef, greeted me cheerfully. "It always smells so good in here!" She said as I helped her carry in my prepared meals for the week. We made quick small talk during the exchange.

After saying goodbye to Cheryl, I inspected the prepared meats and healthy sides before placing them in the refrigerator.

This week's menu consisted of steak pinwheels, roasted cauliflower, and asparagus. Blue Apron had been fun, but the cooking project had not sparked consistency. I went back to the couch and picked up my notepad. I looked around my spotless condo at the floors I did not wax and the windows I did not clean. Cleaning was also on the list of duties I did not make time for and would rather not do. I had a service for that as well.

"Everything but domestic." I said aloud and jotted the words down on the notepad. I thought about Sean and him saying those words to me during our conversation earlier that day.

"You should take this time and consider if this is really what you want." Sean had said.

Our whirlwind relationship had reached serious territories and navigating the new terrain left us both on rocky footing. Our conversation about taking our relationship to the next level had become a steep trek uphill with mutual uncertainty obstructing our ascent.

We looked at each other in silence as I weighed the gravity of the conversation. His words disrupted the stillness. "I love everything about you and us, but if we are going to move forward, I have to know you are all in. Your lifestyle is everything, but domestic. This will be a big change for you."

Two years after the debacle in Italy, I met Sean, a handsome, successful entrepreneur at an evening yacht party. In addition to being fun, attractive, and charismatic. Sean was also a father and the custodial parent to his five-year-old daughter. We had discussed meeting his daughter before, and as it was earlier on in our relationship, my response had been "baby steps". As time went by and our connection deepened, I still did not feel ready for that next step and now it seemed our relationship timeline was no longer an adequate response. For me, it was still too soon. I was leaving for Vegas the next morning and told him I needed the time to think.

I arrived at the Aria Hotel in Las Vegas early the next afternoon. I was excited for the girls' weekend and to spend time with Nomi. Friends since medical school, she and I were close and had a lot in common. She did not have or want children of her own and was in a partnership with a man with kids. After settling into my room, I changed into my black swimsuit with side cut outs and plunging neckline. Adding a sheer burgundy romper, I then slipped on black rhinestone sandals and headed out to the pool to meet Nomi.

"Hey girl hey!" I said cheerfully when I spotted my longtime friend.

Nomi, wearing a green and white striped one shoulder bikini top with matching bottom, stood to greet me. We hugged and laughed.

"It's been too long." She said.

"Yes it has." I agreed.

We ordered drinks and filled each other in on life events. I listened as she told me about her schedule now that they had full custody of their girls. She described the mornings that started before dawn to make breakfast and check on the girls' progress as they readied themselves for school. She then described evenings of preparing dinner and doing homework after a full day of seeing patients in the office. She giggled and then said, "I'm exhausted."

"Sheesh! I bet!" I exclaimed and then asked, "How are you and Vernon?"

"Same old, same old." She replied with a smile. "Between work and the girls there is not much time, but we are ok. Enough about me. How are you?"

We sipped cocktails as I first filled her in on work. I had become disconnected from the title of medical director. The limitations of my role left me with a department barely meeting minimum requirements, and I felt boxed in by excuses and political rhetoric. My expectations for betterment were actively thwarted and I was surrounded by colleagues who were content with the status quo.

I sighed. "The winds of administration have been taken from my sails."

"That does not sound fun at all." Nomi said soothingly and then changed the subject. "What's going on with Sean?"

"Well," I started slowly.

"Uh oh." Nomi said sounding concerned.

"No, it is not bad. Sean is great and he has basically given me an open invitation to be a part of his and his daughter's life." My voice trailed off.

"But." Nomi led, coaxing the rest of the thoughts from my head. "I don't know, Nomi." I shook my head. "Do you remember Tyson?" I asked.

Nomi laughed her distinct and infectious laugh. "Of course, I do." She replied.

"Remember how mad he was when I told him I did not want him moving to Chicago with me?"

"Yep." She responded.

"He was so excited to tell me he had been researching the job market there. As if it were obvious that we were going to Chicago together." I laughed. "I fully expected we would break up when I moved. He was so confused by my confusion." Nomi and I both laughed.

"Navigating a relationship in a new city on top of residency did not make sense to me. Just like with Justin, I chose me over us. Now, I am an established physician administrator and even with all my goals accomplished, and a guy who checks all my boxes, I still feel conflicted."

"It is a lot of work. You have got to want it, otherwise you will not be happy."

I sighed and shook my head. "That's just it, Nomi, I am not sure if I want that type of life at all. Sean is amazing but when he starts talking lifestyle changes and compromise my eyes glaze over."

We continued sipping our drinks as we lay on the cabana shaded from the hot afternoon sun. I thought about Sean. Sean was a great father and a natural nurturer. He described bonding with his little girl via cooking and performing chores together. Sean beamed when speaking of his daughter and the simple joys of his day-to-day life. He reminded me of my own father who worked to cultivate closeness among us all. After my father's death, the rare family time that was shared usually ended in lost tempers and hurt feelings. Dinners were not spent together at a table discussing varying aspects of our days. After cooking, my mother was usually off to work and mealtimes consisted of grabbing a bite and retreating to my room. I was shooed out of the kitchen if I got too close to my mother while she prepared meals and chores were no picnic either. My mother once came at me with a broom when my room was not cleaned to her specifications. When Sean spoke about life with Gracie, I would look at him with a smile, admiring the love he has for his daughter and imagining the childhood I never knew.

Sean had expressed concerns about my readiness for "that level of domestication" and had made mention to my "lifestyle" with trivial commentary regarding prepared meals and my professionally kept home. Initially, it was something we joked and laughed about, now the matter was the crux of our relationship's future. There was validity to his concerns regarding my ability and desire to be a caretaker. I did not have maternal instincts and lacked strong familial bonds. I had not been indoctrinated into the ways of home life and there was not a blank space for which I was waiting with bated breath to write ready-made family. My caretaking skills were limited to teen experiences with babysitting nieces and nephews, and I had been outsourcing household chores for quite some time. It seemed that my upbringing had molded me into someone who was indeed everything except domestic.

I left the cabana and entered the pool. The cool water was soothing against my skin, now a few shades darker despite sunscreen. I dipped into the pool and sat down on a ledge. Water always had a calming effect and helped me to think clearly. "Rosalyn, what do you want?" I said aloud, my chin dipping into the water as I spoke. After Kevin and all my disgust with dating, I was in a good relationship with a good guy. Sean was offering commitment, family, and stability. He was handing me the keys to a life of "happiness" that was everything I was supposed to want. Yet, instead of elation, I felt like a big cat, accustomed to living wild, being presented with a cage. I wanted a life of passion, excitement, and adventure. A life where I could explore any endeavor or fascination at a moment's notice. I wanted to run free.

After a fun filled weekend with Nomi in Vegas, I returned to Chicago where the conversation I needed to have with Sean was waiting for me. With Gracie in her mother's care, Sean arrived at my condo as the sun was setting.

"Hi there." I smiled and greeted Sean with a hug and kiss.

"Hey." He smiled weakly. "How was your trip?" He asked as we walked into my living room and sat on the sofa.

"We had fun. It was great seeing Nomi." I said and paused. Sean looked at me knowing there was more. "I also had some time to think." I gave him a weak smile.

"Let's hear it." He said optimistically.

"You were right. This would be a huge lifestyle change for me as well as a learning curve. I do not have experience being a "family" and we would have to figure it out as we went along."

"Or you could decide that the family life is not for you." He retorted.

"That is also on the spectrum of possibilities." I responded softly. Silence befell the room and the orange hues once decorating the living area were replaced with the dimness of distant streetlights. "I thought a lot about what I want and what is important to me. While I love our connection, we do not want the same things from life, and I am not sure I will be happy if we move forward." I said and the room was once again silent.

After a few minutes of quiet contemplation, Sean responded.

"I cannot risk my feelings growing deeper or allowing my daughter's feelings to get involved."

"I understand, and I would not want you to." I replied nodding in agreement. There was nothing left to be said. We sat in stillness, holding hands in the dark. After a while, I walked him out, and we hugged somberly before closing the door on our relationship.

ABSORBING THE INFORMATION

I stood in the door length mirror and tucked the right side of my new bob behind my ear. The asymmetric style was shorter than I usually wore my hair. Honey brown on top with streaks of the entire blonde to brown spectrum throughout, any movement of my head gave a peek a boo of color. I changed my hair often and my stylist Tina never disappointed. At this most recent appointment, Tina informed me that she was organizing a career panel.

"I am putting together a panel of women in different professions for the young ladies of Wilham's Academy." She told me as I squirmed uncomfortably in the salon chair as she braided down my natural hair.

"If you are available, I would love for you to be on the panel." I reached for my phone and opened my calendar.

"Oh cool, when is it?" I asked awkwardly looking down at my phone while attempting to keep my head at the appropriate angle while Tina continued to work.

"Next Monday." She replied and tilted my head to the other side.

"I am off that day." I replied. Next Monday was an administration day. The new hospital executives continued to extinguish my creative goals for the department, and I had become a puppet, attending meetings, and carrying out their directives. "I would be happy to help." I said after marking the date in my calendar. "What is the panel's focus?" I asked.

"It's a career panel for the juniors and seniors. The panelists are women from several different professions. I would introduce you with a short biography and then you would give more information about your background and your chosen profession. After everyone on the panel has had an opportunity to speak, we will have an open forum for the girls to ask questions." Tina explained, as she continued to braid my hair, twisting my head this way and that.

"Consider it done!" I responded enthusiastically.

"Thanks boo!" Tina said.

After the masterfully created color bomb bob was completed, Tina added, "Think about some advice to give these young ladies. Most of them are from difficult situations. Your story may prove inspiring."

Next Monday had arrived, and I had spent the last week thinking about what words of wisdom I had to impart upon the young ladies of Wilham's Academy. I could tell them about the steps it took to become a doctor, but go to school, study hard, and make good grades sounded generic and uninspiring. While those were the steps to becoming a doctor, there was much more to it than that. There was something else and I could not yet find the words. Sighing, I shook out my bob, grabbed my coat, and headed out the door.

Tina greeted me with a smile as I approached the Wilham's Academy auditorium.

"Thank you so much for joining us today." She beamed and showed me to my place on the panel. I was at one end. I wonder if I will be first or last. I thought to myself as I took my seat and adjusted the nameplate with Dr. Porter written in big bold print.

As the young women started filling the auditorium, I was instantly transported to the halls of Germantown High School. I could almost hear the raucous laughter shared between my friends and I as we lollygagged toward our next class. A few of the young ladies in the auditorium were holding babies in their laps and vivid images of my senior year came to mind. I remembered a few of my senior classmates learning of pregnancies and preparing for young motherhood. I remembered waiting anxiously with one of my best friends as the indicator dye moved rapidly across the small plastic window. I remembered her eyes widening with tears and the sound of her cries as she sobbed in my arms.

Tina started the panel discussion. Each of the panelists were introduced one by one. I was in the seat slated to go last. When speaking of our careers, the panelists, myself included, discussed hard work, discipline, and steadfastness. Some panelists talked about having faith in God while others spoke about identifying support systems. After each panelist spoke, Tina urged the students to be patient, write down their questions, and hold them until after panelist remarks, however the planned format was soon abandoned, and the event became an open forum.

The question-and-answer session began, and I was out of my element. A few of the questions were about parenting. Some questions were directed to the panelists with specific careers. Most of the questions, however, were about love and the navigation of romantic relationships. As the panelists answered questions, I sat pensively at the end of the long table, only half listening to anecdotes about love, communication, and compromise.

I thought about walking away from my relationship with Sean. Those around me were shocked. Even a few of my closest friends did not understand. "What happened?" "You two seemed so happy." The questions were endless, and I was called selfish and scared. I no longer feared a life without traditional companionship, and I learned it was not something I longed for. I had discovered the source of my internal turmoil when dating. I could not prioritize another person over myself and had no desire to seek refuge in a romantic relationship. The only thing that terrified me, was not living the life I wanted. I shrugged off the consistent questions of "What about Sean?" What about him? We discussed our discordance, and the dissolution of our relationship was amicable. I did not need to explain the choices I made to anyone and was not going to tailor my life to fit third party expectations.

"Dr. Porter?" Still partially tuned out, I was startled when Tina said my name. I perked up and smiled at the moderator.

"What final words do you have for these ladies today?"

My pulse quickened. All I had in my head was how sad I was that these young ladies with so much life ahead of them were so focused on romantic relationships. I took a deep breath and swallowed hard. I still did not know what I was going to say when I started speaking.

"First I would like to say thank you for the opportunity to be here and speak with you all." Looking over to my fellow panelists, I said "You have made some excellent points. Hard work and leaning into your support systems cannot be overstated." I turned back to the audience and paused for a moment.

"The advice I have for you is this: Don't be afraid to choose you." I said the words slowly and deliberately, hoping to mask the trembling in my voice as I said them. "I challenge everyone in this room to get to know yourselves. Learn what you like and do not like. Understand and embrace your perceived flaws and fall completely in love with yourself. When you do that, the questions about who likes you and who does not will no longer matter. Decide what you want your life to look like outside of anyone else's opinion or consideration and chase that life fervently." I could hear the urgency in my voice as the words spilled out of my mouth.

When I finished speaking, I was met with silence and Tina quickly moved on to the next panelist. I was sure my words had been unpopular, but I hoped that someone in the audience needed to hear them. If just one of those girls absorbed any of what I said and felt inspired to choose self or to chase a dream, then it was worth saying.

The panelist discussion left me thinking about my life and my choices as I drove home. As a young girl, I was more spice than sugar. I am now a direct and outspoken woman. The loss of my father and being raised by a tiger mom forced me to learn to self-soothe. I am now a woman that does not look externally for acceptance or validation. I found cats as a girl and had grown into a woman with feline traits and a loner nature. Daddy's little daredevil had grown to be a woman with that same longing for adventure. At the age of ten, I discovered my body and learned how to escape both sleeping and waking nightmares and had become a woman who reveled in her sexuality. I am a woman who still lived by the words my father gave me long ago. I can do whatever I want.

It had been three years since I audaciously stood before the senior staff at Park Lawn Hospital and demanded change in departmental leadership. I told them, "This institution deserves better, and I will gladly take on the responsibility." I was tenacious, well prepared, and balanced in the combined roles of colleague and administrator. Working closely with the veteran nursing director, obstetrical volume increased, and departmental metrics improved. Standards of patient care were elevated, and my team of physicians rose to the occasion. It was disappointing to see the department I worked so hard to improve backslide into mediocrity fueled by lackluster indifference. Now that the role had become a passionless endeavor, it was time for a new adventure. A plan started to crystallize in my mind.

By the time I arrived home, the decision had been made. I would take my own advice and continue fervently chasing my dreams. With a clear vision of the life I wanted, I went to my office and opened my computer. I navigated to my work email account and started to type.

Dear Sir,

Please allow this letter to serve as my resignation notice from Park Lawn Hospital and The Medical Group. I am resigning my position to pursue other interests. I want to sincerely thank you for all the time and effort put into helping me to become the physician that I am today. I also want to express gratitude for the opportunity to serve as Chair and Medical Director of Obstetrics at Park Lawn Hospital. The experience gained via my administrative role is immeasurable.

I understand that my resignation will cause a disruption, and I will do everything in my power to facilitate a smooth transition for any replacement. After my departure, if you need to contact me for any reason, please refer to the attached contact card. Your calls and emails will always be welcome to me.

Regards,

Rosalyn Porter, M.D.

I leaned back in the office chair and reviewed the drafted email. As I addressed the message, memories of the moments working at Park Lawn Hospital flooded my mind. My nurses called me Dr. Feisty. It was an endearing moniker I received for being a fierce advocate for patients and fellow caregivers. I had become friends with many of the nurses on staff and had a deep respect for my physician colleagues. I would miss my team. I smiled wistfully and clicked send.

SPHINX AND THE CAT LADY

"Thanks for joining me!" I said excitedly to Megan as she entered my car.

"No problem." Megan responded and settled into the passenger seat. The news that I quit my job and was leaving Chicago had stunned Megan. Megan responded to my announcement with congratulatory words, but I could hear the sadness in her voice. My plan was rapidly progressing, and I had less than four months left in Chicago. The road trip to the cat breeder provided an opportunity for us to catch up.

"I cannot believe you are leaving Chicago!" Megan shouted and nudged my side playfully.

I laughed. "I know! It has been twelve years. I am excited for the change."

"So, where to next?" Megan asked.

"Next stop, Nashville!" I exclaimed and filled her in on my plans.

After sending notice of my resignation, I checked my personal email to find a recruitment letter from a hospitalist group specializing in obstetrical care. I clicked the link which navigated me to the company's website. As a hospitalist physician, I would care for and evaluate patients in an emergency setting. There would be no office practice nor administrative responsibilities. I would work in shifts, which ultimately meant more free time and the flexibility to pursue other endeavors. The description of the fast-paced patient care environment suited my strengths of being a quick thinker who was cool under pressure. The more I read about the position, the more confident I became that this was the job I wanted.

Taking a position with the hospitalist group would allow me to focus solely on patient care and rediscover the reasons I chose obstetrics. With a full-time schedule comprised of seven twenty-four hour shifts monthly, I would have ample time to pursue the lifestyle I wanted. I wanted a life of travel, adventure, and creative pursuits. I wanted to work so that I could live, not have my career stifle me into stagnation. With programs in thirty-two states, the organization was large, and there were several locations to choose from.

Chicago had been my haven and a safe space; however, it always felt temporary, and I was not inextricably linked to the city. After surviving Chicago's brutal winter weather for over ten years, I wanted milder winters and hotter summers. I had self-isolated, lived by my own rules, and used my time in Chicago to heal the scars of my youth. No longer needing a refuge, I wanted to be closer to friends and chosen family. I wanted community. I wanted to feel rooted. I wanted to feel home. I responded to the recruitment email and inquired about the opening in Nashville, Tennessee. Within days, the recruiter responded to my message and a week later I flew out for interviews. When the organization made me an offer, I happily accepted.

"That happened so fast." Megan mused.

"It did, but once I decided the job was more exhausting than fulfilling, letting it go was easy." I responded.

"I don't think I could just walk away from my job like that." Megan continued.

"You enjoy your work, so hopefully that is a decision you will not have to make." I replied.

"First Sean, now Chicago!" Megan said teasing.

I snickered. "I chose me. My life has taught me that if I do not put myself first and chase what makes me happy, no one else will."

In my relationship with Sean, I tried desperately to fit the mold of life partner. Every day I continued to feel like a square peg being forced into a round hole. Every day I tried to suppress the conflicting emotions. Every day I wondered if this would be the day that I would really want *it*. The day I would want that dangling carrot of a life surrounded by a picketed fence. That day never came, and when I broke up with Sean, the narrative of what I was supposed to want faded away.

"All I can say is I no longer want to be an administrator and I don't want to be a wife." I said candidly. Megan observed me thoughtfully. "You may not fully understand, but every decision I make is to make *me* happy."

While continuing the drive, I told Megan about my new home. Joy connected me with a Nashville realtor and after a conversation about what I wanted and where, Catherine found the perfect place. Only five minutes away from my soon to be place of employment, the new construction townhome was just what I wanted. The only standalone town house in the picturesque complex, the spacious two-bedroom, two-and-a-half-bathroom unit was offset from the rest and had its own private courtyard. I was able to choose flooring, countertops, tiles, and paint, customizing the space. I planned to create a bright and inspiring writing room and turn a part of the huge garage into a home gym. It was the first place I would live that was mine, and I was ecstatic.

We pulled up to the cat breeder's home and I squealed with excitement. "We are here!"

"You and your cats!" Megan said shaking her head and chuckling.

Beaming from ear to ear as we exited the car and walked up to the house, I only laughed in response to Megan's comment. When I recounted the tribulations of my past, the importance of cats could not be overstated. Kitt, Frizz, Siegfried, and Sox had all been strays who magically appeared in my time of need. Kitt and Frizz were my childhood companions and they taught me to be curious and frisky. Siegfried was unruly and surly, however comforted me with cuddles during all night study sessions while in medical school. Sox barged into my life during residency and her distant, yet loving nature made her a fast favorite. Cats were not a substitute for the children I did not want. They were more than that. Cats had become a part of my chosen family and a reflection of myself.

After the grief of losing Sox dissipated, I researched cat breeds and fell in love with the Bengal. Beautiful cats with spotted coats and athletic bodies, Bengals closely resemble wild cats. They are playful animals that need space to run and jump. Bengals are vocal and have an affinity for water. The more I read about Bengals the more I developed a kinship with the animal. When I found a silver and black spotted beauty that needed a home, I knew I had to have her.

The breeder handed me the four-month-old Bengal kitten, and the cat swiped its paw at my face in response.

"My type of kitty!" I said with a smirk.

"She's gorgeous!" Megan said and then asked, "What are you going to name her?"

"Her name is Sphinx." I responded and cuddled the kitten close to my chest.

The Sphinx, a mythical creature of Egyptian origin, has a face of a human or a cat, the body of a lion, and the wings of a falcon. In mythology, the Sphinx were fierce and oftentimes malevolent protectors of ancient cities and the mysteries within. In Greek culture, for the Sphinx to grant one access to the city of Thebes a riddle had to be answered. Those who did not answer correctly met a violent end.

I was riddled with questions and filled with confusion following my breakup with Kevin. The fiasco in Italy forced me to ponder third party perspectives of my personhood. I was compelled to consider my characteristics in aggregate and develop a deeper understanding of my life's journey. Through the lens of self-reflection, I discovered that RP, born out of abandonment and grief, had been my guardian and protector shielding my softer side from the perils of the world. I solved my bucket box riddle and discovered that I have always been the gatekeeper to my happiness. As I held the mewing kitten close, thinking about my journey of self-discovery, I knew that Sphinx was the perfect name for my new feline friend.

The remaining months in Chicago passed quickly. On the day of my departure, I stood looking at the empty condo and reminisced on the life I built in the windy city. I remembered the joy and excitement I had when I first moved to the West Loop. I remembered the drunken nights and laughter shared between myself and friends. I remembered passionate romps with lovers. I remembered the hard work of pursuing departmental leadership. Nostalgia washed over me. Chicago had left its mark, but it was time to move on. I placed the keys to the condo in the kitchen drawer and took one last look at the city skyline from the twenty first floor corner unit. As I closed the door behind me, headed to embark upon a new chapter in my life, I felt the tingle of butterflies.

ON A SUNNY AND WARM FALL DAY IN NASHVILLE, I LOUNGED outside on the spacious deck of my new home. The scene surrounding me was serene. I swayed back and forth in the oversized chair; my legs rested on an ottoman with my Microsoft Z Book in my lap. Birds chirped in the luscious trees and a gentle breeze brushed against leaves that had not yet started to turn.

Sphinx, curled up next to me, purred contently. My new job was going well, and I had settled into my new home. In the upcoming months, I had travel plans for Bali, Indonesia, Rio de Janeiro, Brazil, and I would be spending the new year with Allen in Ghana. I had reconnected with my sisters and their families, I was closer to Nomi and Chris, and Joy lived right around the corner. I was finally home.

My curiosity about gender expectations and the cat lady trope led to a deeper exploration of self. Chronicling my journey to living life on my terms gave me an appreciation for the trials of my life and allowed me to fuse RP and Rosalyn together as one. I felt complete. I was no longer suppressing the vulnerability that lives within and had found strength in the characteristic. I no longer believed that sharing my story was pathetic, and I was proud of the woman that I had become. I was proud to have fulfilled the promise to my father. I was proud that I survived my adolescence. I was proud that I did not succumb to depression, anger, or fear, and that at a young age I made the decision to thrive. I picked up scars during my teens and as a young woman I learned to embrace those perceived flaws. I was proud of my unwavering sense of individuality and for constantly refusing to let the narratives of third parties become my story.

As I continued to enjoy the breeze, I considered the stories of the crazy cat lady and realized they were not narratives of her own making. Maybe, she has been misperceived and was not a sullen someone who had fallen short of societal expectations. Maybe, like me, she had chosen the road less traveled. Maybe, she chose to define happiness for herself disregarding the opinions of others. I envisioned myself as an old woman with a multitude of memories, and I saw bookshelves lined with tales of my many grand adventures. I welcomed becoming an old woman surrounded by cats, feeling fulfilled and satisfied having lived life on my terms. A life filled with an abundance of love shared with reconnected blood relatives, close friends, the Grays, and chosen family.

I took a deep breath and was overcome with an enormous sense of gratitude. I had searched my heart, and I knew where I had been and where I wanted to go. I was thankful to have learned what excited me about life and about love and I was proud of myself for choosing to live the life I wanted. In the ultimate fusion of strength and vulnerability, I decided I would tell my story. A story of finding solace in solitude. A story of fate and felines. A story of triumph over tribulations. A story filled with self-love and no regrets.

"Here goes!" I said aloud with equal parts excitement and trepidation. I opened my laptop, placed my hands on the keyboard and started to type.

> Chapter 1 Italy here we ~~cum~~ come!
> *You have got to be kidding me! Storming down the hallway towards the elevator, this thought repeated over and over in my mind as I forcefully pressed the down button. Flashes of what just transpired were on instant replay, forcing me to relive the rebuff. "I cannot fucking believe this!"...*

END

REFERENCES

Bartholomew, K; Horowitz, L. M. (1991). Attachment styles among young adults: A test of a four-category model, Journal of Personality and Social Psychology, Vol 61, pp. 226-244, doi:10.1037/0022-3514.61.2.226, PsycINFO Database Record

Baumrind, D. (1991). Parenting styles and adolescent development. In J. Brooks-Gunn, R. Lerner, A.C. Peterson (Eds.), The Encyclopaedia of Adolescence (746-758). New York: Garland.

Budiansky, Stephen The Character of Cats: The Origins, Intelligence, Behavior And Stratagems Of Felis Silvestris Catus By Date Published 2002-06-03

Capps, D. The Decades of Life: Relocating Erikson's Stages. Pastoral Psychology 53, 3–32 (2004). https://doi.org/10.1023/B:PASP.0000039322.53775.2b

Collins, N. L., & Read, S. J. (1990). Adult attachment, working models, and relationship quality in dating couples. Journal of Personality and Social Psychology, 58(4), 644–663. https://doi.org/10.1037/0022-3514.58.4.644

Crawford, M., & Popp, D. (2003) Sexual double standards: A review and methodological critique of two decades of research,

The Journal of Sex Research, 40:1, 13-26, DOI: 10.1080/00224490309552163

Darwall-Smith, Robin. "Emperors and Architecture: A Study of Flavian Rome." (1996).

Gordon, Rachel A et al. "Physical attractiveness and the accumulation of social and human capital in adolescence and young adulthood: assets and distractions." Monographs of the Society for Research in Child Development vol. 78,6 (2013): 1-137. doi:10.1002/mono.12060

Hadingham, E. Uncovering Secrets of the Sphinx. Smithsonian Magazine. Feb. 2010.

Horst, E. A. "Reexamining Gender Issues in Erikson's Stages of Identity and Intimacy." Journal of Counseling and Development vol. 73,3 (1995): 271-8 https://doi.org/10.1002/j.1556-676.1995.tb01748.x

McLeod, S. A. (2008). Erik Erikson | Psychosocial Stages - Simply Psychology. Retrieved from http://www.simplypsychology.org/Erik-Erikson.html

McRobbie, L. R. (2017) The Crazy History of the Cat Lady. Boston Globe. Web. 2 May 2021.

Mueller, T. Secrets of the Colosseum: A German archaeologist has finally deciphered the Roman amphitheater's amazing underground labyrinth. Smithsonian Magazine. Jan. 2011.

Petmd.com. 2021. Bengal House Cat Cat Breed Hypoallergenic, Health and Life Span | PetMD. [online] Available at: <https://www.petmd.com/cat/breeds/c_ct_bengal> [Accessed 3 May 2021].

Shaver, P. R., & Hazan, C. (1993). Adult romantic attachment: Theory and evidence. In D. Perlman& W. Jones (Eds.), Advances in personal relationships (Vol. 4, pp. 29± 70). London: Jessica Kingsley Publishers

Sheff E. Polyamorous Women, Sexual Subjectivity and Power. Journal of Contemporary Ethnography. 2005;34(3):251-283. doi:10.1177/0891241604274263

Wikipedia contributors. "Sphinx." Wikipedia, The Free Encyclopedia. Wikipedia, The Free Encyclopedia, 25 Apr. 2021. Web. 2 May. 2021.

Wong. A. Et al. The Review of The Ugly Truth and Negative Aspects of Online Dating. Global Journal of Management And Business Research, [S.l.], may 2015. ISSN 2249-4588. Available at: <https://www.journalofbusiness.org/index.php/GJMBR/article/view/1700>. Date accessed: 03 May 2021.

ACKNOWLEDGMENTS

I want to thank Amirah Cook, my mentor, for all of your support and encouragement throughout the process of creating this book. You are such a positive light and meeting you in Bali was life changing. Your words have been priceless and I am forever grateful.

Jarrell Cook, thank you for the amazing cover art. You captured the essence of Rosalyn and RP perfectly and I could not be more proud to have my work encased in your own.

Joy, thank you for your beautiful foreword. You have known me since before I knew myself. Thank you for being my ace through all the versions of me. Thank you for always seeking to understand without judgement. I can always count on you to see me. I love you.

Tonya, my boo, I love you for getting me. Thank you for knowing what I needed and for introducing me to Amirah via Instagram. That trip to Bali solidified our sisterhood and I thank you for supporting my dreams.

Fawzia, thank you for your friendship. Thank you for understanding and supporting my decisions for change. Thank you for reminding me to do what my heart compels me to even when I am afraid.

To my sisters, thank you all for allowing me to learn from you. Thank you for being safe places when I needed them.

To my Holy Cross Family Birth Center family, I miss you dearly. Thank you for allowing me to grow. Thank you for supporting both Dr. Feisty and Rosalyn.

To Shelonda Richardson, thank you for your sharp and honest feedback. You believed in the project from the beginning and I appreciate your time and support.

To Andrew B. Marshall, thank you for the conversations that always dive deeper than the surface. Thank you for believing in the power of my story.

ABOUT THE AUTHOR

Starr, M.D. is the pen name for Dr. Rosalyn Porter. Rosalyn is a board certified obstetrician and gynecologist. Originally from Memphis, TN, Rosalyn became the first doctor in her family when she received her medical degree from Vanderbilt University. She completed her residency training at University of Chicago Medical Center and went on to practice obstetrics and gynecology in Chicago for 12 years. Currently Rosalyn lives in Nashville, TN with her cats, Sphinx and Isis, where she continues to practice medicine and writes creative nonfiction. In her spare time, Rosalyn indulges in adrenaline filled activities, spends time with loved ones, and travels the world. In her ongoing love affair with life, Rosalyn chases her dreams fervently and encourages those around her to do the same.

CPSIA information can be obtained
at www.ICGtesting.com
Printed in the USA
BVHW070933301221
625049BV00018B/310